# Poems Recycled

## – IRENE EARIS –

An environmentally friendly book printed and bound in England by
www.printondemand-worldwide.com

**Mixed Sources**
Product group from well-managed
forests, and other controlled sources
www.fsc.org  Cert no. TT-COC-002641
© 1996 Forest Stewardship Council

**FSC**

**PEFC**
PEFC/16-33-415

PEFC Certified
This product is
from sustainably
managed forests
and controlled
sources
www.pefc.org

This book is made entirely of chain-of-custody materials

www.fast-print.net/store.php

Poems Recycled
Copyright © Irene Earis 2012

ISBN 978-178035-520-7

First published 2012 by
FASTPRINT PUBLISHING
Peterborough, England.

The poems here are recycled in the sense that they have been gradually accruing in folders and gathering dust for many years. But now, in the spirit of the times, I decided to clear some of them off my shelves and send them out into the world in a new form via a web site (www.poemsrecycled.co.uk) in the hope that someone else might gain some pleasure from them. The poems are also contained here in this slim volume for those who might prefer to read a printed version.

I have loved poetry all my life since my father read me his favourite poems from various old-fashioned anthologies, in particular one called 'Laurel and Gold', when I was a little girl after the war. I went on to read English at university, teach English and hang around at the edges of the poetry scene, attending festivals and local readings and sending in poems to competitions. But I never managed to find a way through to publication, except for a few random poems.

I am now in my sixties and have accumulated hundreds of poems over the years, so this is my solution – to publish a small selection of them on the web and in this short volume.

Thank you for reading this far!

## Puzzling about Life

*Studying literature brought me in contact with many different views on life and I have always enjoyed reading books and attending courses on philosophy, religion, psychology and history. Ultimately, however, I realised that the brain alone and its accumulated knowledge cannot answer the important questions about living on earth – though they can take one a long way and continue to provide checks and balances.*

## Adaptations of the Atom

If you have known the rare,
the fine-art moment,
which no words can snare,
which no precise defining clauses
can encapsulate,

the moment when the same
constituents that
form the linear frame,
the time-bound boundaries we tread like
water, startlingly

re-form, switch and melt
kaleidoscoping
into newness, transform
into strange arrangements, unpredicted
emphases and highlights -

a quickly tidied room,
a light dispersing
long accustomed gloom,
a few strokes of a painter's brushwork
making instant landscape -

and if within that space
of re-creating
seconds you can trace
the infinite potential, sense
the flexibility

of cells, the adaptations
of the atom, its
hidden fluctuations
for secret pointillist effects,
shifting the solid world

over and again
in and out of
beauty, health and pain,
moulded by power of will and thought
in an overwhelming instant,

you know that nothing is
impossible
that everything is
real but also variable
by purposeful desire,

not illusory
but never fixed,
so that excitedly
you step out daily on to rock
consumable by fire.

## Making Sense of God

No one can make sense of God.
He is a language no one understands.
She is a distant voice you have
to strain to hear,
a close-up shot that blurs because too near.

His handwriting cannot be read
however much you puzzle over it,
guessing from context. Her sounds on tape
distort and change –
the more you hear, the more you find them strange.

Somewhere there are words to pin
him down in black and white, technical
vocabulary, the right turn
of phrase, on the tip
of my tongue, a temporary memory slip.

Somewhere, through some lens, in some
laboratory, under some laser
beam, by some new type of X-ray, surely
he can be seen
or registered on some computer screen.

Infuriatingly unwilling
to be revealed; missing while present;
a philosophical conundrum;
she stretches the mind
like a landscape painting offered to the blind.

I try to recall his tune, her scent.
Her silhouette passed by my window far
too fast to see. I know his name
(or pseudonym)
but never can quite put a face to him.

## Free Will

How must it feel as an artist,
faultless in technique
and brilliant in conception,
performing at a constant level of perfection,
yet having to accept that your unique
masterpieces must be free
to change themselves at will,
perversely to dull or flake their paint until
their impact fades, the lines slip out of harmony;
that the careful products of your talents
may disorder themselves, choose to fail,
resist the pull back into balance?

How must it feel as a poet
burning with a ringing
declamation, that combines
thought and image in a magic of mantric lines,
to let the words shuffle away from singing,
from the bold glow of resonance,
the layered niceness of the just phrase,
self-deprecatingly to cloak themselves in a haze
of cliche and deliberate dissonance,
to limp and halt without exertion,
shrinking apologetically in fear
before the strong role of musical assertion?

How must it feel as a God
initiating worlds,
ideals and aspirations,
beautiful complex human creations,
philosophical utopias,
yet letting them be undermined,
received with embarrassment, fragmented,
dismissed with disbelief, endlessly prevented
from achievement; to find
that your inventions tend
to prefer an easy imperfection,
compassion, not admiration, in the end?

## Wind

This sudden change of weather,
boisterous wind ransacking
and upheaving the neat gardens,
romping and scattering wreckage
over the metalled roads,
makes me delight again
in all disordered doubts,
buffeting conventions
and tossing leaves of assumption
in crackling heaps of protest,
or in the fields of mind
exposing the dark soil
and the creatures underneath,
stirring a path for growth;
no settled, sculptured landscape
of Newtonian measured calm,
where predicted figures move
unruffled and prepared,
but a gusty, shifting sky
different from every view,
a relative universe
for each who cares to look.
Sun soothes, but can stun,
too, our sense of awe;
while in the flurrying force
and uncertain potential of wind
truths and doubts can merge,
cloud-gaps shoot out shafts

and mysteries blow in our eyes.

## My Poem, My Life

This is my poem – my life;
rearranging the challenges and duties
into rhythm and resonance;
unravelling the chores and dissonance
into a prosody of love;
transplanting from the rife exuberance
of metaphor the seeding image
proliferating into dominance.

On the page, a selective world,
an angled snapshot of reality;
in reality, a selective angle
snapped by my artist self
to illustrate my mood, my theme, my tone
now and again, from here and there,
making the world my own.

I can choose light or dark,
satire or celebration,
sardonic insecurity
or the liberation
of self-asserting wonder.
It is my poem, my life.
As I imagine, so I am.
Through conscious ideation
the rough matter of the universe allows
genuine co-creation.

For poets in the barrenness of silence
giving birth with words
to unique aspects of soul
in new bodies of cadence
is a patch of perfection,
bliss in brackets,
in a context of incoherence.

But to shape and form my life
from an endless inner source of power,
daily amending, smoothing, excising,
responding to the beat within
as it fluctuates on all dimensions,
is to be a force of nature,
a surfboard rider on the switchback tides of living,
adapting, controlling, improvising
to harmonise myself within the flow;
is to be such an artist
that my whole existence is a poem in process,
a long instant of exhilaration,
outworking inspiration,
daily deftness of metric variation
that only gods, I used to think, could know.

## Questions and Answers

Give me the answers to all
my questions. I'm mad to grasp
awareness, to seize cognition,
to possess more consciousness;
agog with curiosity,
dizzy with desire
to know, to understand
life, God, everything.
Tell me. Explain. Share.
Why are the secrets withheld?

Until the apple tree
sends its roots down searching in darkness;
lifts its branches outwards, upwards;
waits, reflecting, through the rainstorm;
lingeringly absorbs the light;
experiences through every surface
of sensing leaf and steadfast bark;
the apples will not ripen.
Tying apples to your boughs
will not make them yours

## Creative Energy

Whatever energy it is
that goes on making worlds,
it clearly loves its acts
of ingenuity.
Its spurts of creativity
must give perpetually
such clenches of excitement,
such glad reliefs
of energy released,
it cannot stop, but still attracts
fresh matter to be grouped
and sculpted endlessly,
with inexhaustible
originality. It is
addicted to the joy of it.
Each new uniqueness,
fresh-materialised, must draw
it on and generate
the power for more and more.

Why otherwise is every stone,
here at the stream, a shape
and colour all its own?
Shades of orange, brown and green,
of grey and black, blend
in harmony and yet amaze
with different combinations.
This one is straight and square
and quite alone; this rock,
forming the bank, seems to have grown
here from the start of time;
this, carved in a maze
of Celtic knotwork;
this a golden honeycomb,
a solid net of cells;
this one sketched in filigree
of free-hand scratching,
and this a mottled egg
that ossified before the hatching.

Knowing the electric thrill,
the inner stir and murmur
at the exercise of skill
to form one small, unique
collaboration of language
on an empty page,
the endless constant heaps
and piles of fresh creation
that our world consists of
can bemuse and fill
us with repletion of amazement;
yet also must presage
a wonder of security
knowing how much an artist
cherishes her work
and goes on whittling at it –
not from need or duty
but only for further subtler shades
and layers of deeper beauty.

## Input of the Mysterious

There is an impulse,
an instant beacon-flash across the darkness
that you might blink and miss;

a declaration of colour
from a crystal as the gaze shifts
or the sun appears to move;

infinitesimal electric charge
from ether, registered
as a hint of feeling.

It can be ignored,
overlaid by life's distractions,
but may pulse again,

or pulse again in memory
and start a sequence, a spread
of static in the brain,

a slight shock of redirection,
minute jarring of the compass,
a tilt to the tiller.

Stars blaze and die
throughout the universe. We only know
after millennia.

These are the scintillations
I close my eyes to see; open my sails
for the breaths of this breeze;

to move my clogged thoughts out of matter
and my morass of days
out of heaviness,

to tune my life to the pitch
of a higher scale heard only in silence,
to submit to the weight of a whisper,

to be driven by a dream,
a spark through the fog, and changed by a Face
seen once in chaotic crowd.

## Transformation Expected

Some brooding days my eyes richly unfocus;
household objects break into atoms, waver
to translucence.

Slowly I reach towards these concentrations
of frozen light and energy, expecting
no resistance.

Compositions readily re-form,
angular permutations simultaneously
eliding.

Verticals bend like rubber, horizontals
undulate and every cell trembles towards
the invisible.

A leaf looms glossy and solid, wisps into
a filigree of veins, switches to a photograph
in negative.

At any moment I shall be clairvoyant,
stare astonished into other worlds, see earth
etherealise.

The quickening suspense sharpens the senses.
The universe vibrates with shifting clusters
of potential.

The next breathless intake of my breath
will loose a flood of meaning, final explanation,
transformation

# Meditation

*I was brought up to attend church in an orthodox way but left in my early twenties. However, meditation and prayer have continued to be important to me, for healing myself and others and as a way to explore inner states. These poems reflect some of my experiences of meditation.*

## Happiness

When, for a still moment,
the million lives lived
in the head are lost
in the one lived in the moment -

when the worlds behind the eyes
forfeit their independence,
run in a single channel
and pour into real acts -

when, by a sudden healing
concentration, the sea
parts, disclosing the deep
iceberg floating entire -

when frustration with one span
of the countless possible
drains away, sense of brevity
recedes in a surge of wholeness -

## Bypassing Death

Bypassing death
I simply circumambulate
its wrench and fearful strangeness,
even now in life slipping,
with a little motive power of will,
into other vibrant states,
future full existences
but now mere sun-filled holidays
that rouse into richer realness
leaving a memory more dear and clear
than whole years of time's existence
greyly recalled.

Bypassing death
briefly, on inner outings, I explore
landscapes of healing harmony;
scenes of wisdom, art and insight that stir
and ignite the mind; meetings with friends;
extracts of living that presume
total unknown worlds;
states of intensity of light
where sound and sight
in rarefied brilliance
refract as if through water
to the straining sense.

Bypassing death
I know, surely from felt experience,
that through death's centre
I shall move off freely
into this enhancement,
the enlargement of this vividness -
always close, always reachable.
I live my dull days here
within its scent, its consciousness,
its memory, as of loved ones
absent for an hour, calmly certain
of reunion.

## Peace

Lying in sunlight in a garden is a short route to the celestial.
Once, for instance, I moved
through bright vibrancy, through resonating aureoles of sunlight,
into every kind of peace.

The peace that issues not from silence
but familiar background modulations
of uninvolving birdsong, or the drip and drop of water,
or papers rustling at another library desk.

The peace, while lying in long grass,
after distracted thought, of finding every sense absorbed
in the infra-structure of grass-blades,
a living labyrinth of mazing lattice.

The peace when you think music has ended
but strain, hopeful, doubtful, for perhaps another almost silent
chord.

Peace of release from labour, pain, testing.

Peace of certainty after lingering ambiguity.

Peace of security, the sureness of the falsity of fear.

Peace in the willed stillness of the body
amongst the busy transience of nature.
Peace in such exertion of the body
as wipes the mind clean of identity.

Peace, descending slow and fearless into water
and breathing on into the depths.
Peace, floating wingless and without direction,
heavy and relaxed among the clouds.
Peace with the body radiantly aflame
and the self wreathing upwards in a constant lifting.
And peace in the dark chambers of the supporting earth.

All these states and dynasties of peace
subtly shading, overlapping indefinably,
in a moment I experienced for aeons –
except no longer I –
pure personification of the abstract of peace
the emotion of peace
peace through the senses
peace through abstaining from the senses
and yet some point of self, as in dreams, still left to marvel,
"So this is Nirvana, Irene.
This is how the drop feels in the ocean.
Tat tvam asi. You are That."

And I was in my garden chair again, and late afternoon,
in shadow since the sun had moved behind the house,
and the moon, almost full, rising into day blueness,
the Wesak moon, Buddha face of pale beneficence,
nodding in satisfaction, wise and self-contained,
with its sleight of smile.

## In This Empty House

In this empty house
I find myself significant. My feet
now move momentously. The echoes beat
against the vacant watching walls and fill
the indrawn pause of silence at my will
in this empty house.

Opening a door
involves suspense and caution; hinges creak,
vistas swing to sight. But should I speak
the crash and blare of words as I began
would agitate more speculations than
opening a door.

Walking up the stair
I venture round this interim retreat
and feel enclosing emptiness complete
my sense of separateness. Each breath I take
makes the air tremble, makes the dust shake,
walking up the stair.

Leaving the house at last
I breathe again the merging muddled race
that infiltrates the isolated space
diffusing all the quiet. Demands bombard
the fragile hoarded fragments that I guard,
leaving the house at last.

In this empty house
the silence waits for those who turn the key.
Unbroken sunlight slants for all to see
who enter. The rewards are high but few -
detachment and a sudden inward view
in this empty house.

## Within

Between the right and the left of me,
enlightenment and ignorance,
good and evil,
the real and the unreal,
between my two eyes
between my two lungs
between the twin pillars of darkness and light,
in this valley of being between two ridges
lies the landscape without horizon,
the silent sky without a cloud
the quiet night without a star
the restful bliss of emptiness.

Away from the distracting pulls and clamour,
chaos of images and clash of colour,
ties of the body and bondage of the hour
lies the still void
always
uncreated, formless,
where self loses itself in power
where with relief I am no longer me
where I am
where I am free.

## Moving about in Worlds not Realised

Water and sunlight.
The overflowing and the permeation.

With eyes lifted and closed
towards the sun,
the mountain stream pounding and pouring
at my side,
I sense the earth's true form –
unfixed perfection
in the world of true reality.

In the bright deafening
of the moment,
first the etheric garden,
then the moorland roughness
focuses more clearly;
then they mingle
in blissful dual consciousness.

We fail to realise
the worlds we move in
here on earth until
an incursion of sunlight,
a heartcry or half-reverie
links us in a hurl
of comprehension, a swirl
of recognition that whirls on
and leaves us grounded again –
but richer and more secure,
smiling in several worlds,
each just as sure.

## Cottage Megaliths

A day of walking, laughing, eating, talking.
Then, late in the evening, we decide
to meditate. No formality.
Four of us in a Welsh cottage by fire
and candle light. Stillness and silence. Only
the burning logs shuffling, turning over
occasionally as if in sleep. Very
distant, the stream's persistent sibilation.

Afterwards, opening my eyes before the others,
from my low chair they are dark
rocks, megaliths, ultra-human,
with the inner tension and self-absorption of stone;
identical in substance to their species
yet curiously outstanding by their conscious
placement, the contrivance of their point
within the landscape where, deep underground,
they link by streams of hidden energy
to greater powers, mutely working and shaping,
forces ungraspable by mind or words.

The tiny room, low-beamed and smoky, darkens
as the fire, the outer light, nods low.
The human stones are drawing clarity
and daylight from the worlds they watch within.
Then, slowly, one by one, each stirs
blinking and smiling, focussing back into dimness,
the murky strangeness of the human room.

## Heaven and Earth

When banks of cloud have rolled aside
and I have slowly stepped out through the rift
into dawning sun,
and felt my heavy body glide into warm totality of being, drift
into blueness
of gentle smiles and dazzled filling
in summer space miles above sky; and living
is a sparkling
stillness rising up and spilling
over from receiving into giving,
then I never
wish to wrench myself away
back into limitation, greyness and decay.

When I observe in meditation
mountains, buildings, gardens in my mind,
and suddenly
I step through the mirror of creation
beyond the screen I watch, and find
I can fully live
and move in these realities,
experience events quite unforeknown,
be taken firmly
through strange towns and territories
to see new art and buildings and be shown
great beings
deep in council; then I descend
reluctantly to earth when visions end.

Yet sometimes when I think of earth
from far beyond its stains and agony
I see what love,
what tenderness is given birth
by all the pain and the disharmony.
A mother needs
her troubled child to soothe. The candle
needs the darkness. I hurry back towards
disorder, rolling
up my sleeves, eager to handle
my corner of the chaos. For love's rewards
are instant here.
Compassion needs suffering in the end,
and beauty and truth a broken world to mend.

## My Church

No walls, no roof,
but a stillness enclosed as I duck inside,
a sudden seeing as my eyes adjust.
Underused, empty, needing no key,
it travels with me wherever I go,
a private chapel for me alone.

No priests, no bishops.
A church made of air. Non-conformist
but making no protest. Shape-shifting, changing,
it can't be divisive. Free-moving, free-thinking,
I do my own asking and give my own thanks.
The world is my bible and silence my creed.

No pulpits, no preaching,
but disestablished and truly catholic;
unconditional and undeserved.
No frustrations involved in its ritual,
no rules or restrictions, no petty conventions;
blasphemy meaningless, heresy void.

No organs, no hymnbooks.
I make my own music, resounding with freedom,
released from old bonds. And all that I value
from a life's observation I use for my praises;
everything read and admired is my prayerbook;
my icons and images, family and friends.

A tough church,
this quiet invisible centre of certainty.
It steps over death as a minor obstacle;
it gathers no mice nor owls in its belfries.
Vivid as light through a stained-glass window,
intense as darkness in a hermit's cave.

No buttresses needed
to prop and to strengthen. This is a church
indestructible, given not made;
knowing that everything always, already,
is part of the godhead, so cannot be separate,
cannot be severed or left to fade.


Part of the Word
that was spoken in darkness commanding the cosmos,
the flow of the infinite epic sung
from the start of the world. And to blend with its metre
in consciousness, this is my worship, to light up
its cadence with love in my line of the verse.

## Persephone

They say I only loved the bright, defined
worlds of flowers and light. True, I screamed
as I was pulled below through the ravine,
the chasm depth into the underworlds.
But that was shock. Earth shuddered over me
in darkness, just as I felt reconciled
at last to all its simple limitations,
its childish consolations, the hard and solid
world my mother bore me into, denying
any other. Yet, in fact, since first
I thought at all I longed for deeper things.
Behind my eyes, I turned to rich, warm
caves of night, wished to linger in
the velvet, textured shadows of my dreams,
slip sideways through the beckoning cracks between
waking and unconsciousness. Never
could I believe that grass and sky might bound
reality. It seemed a superficial
game to me, a diagram of life,
an outline sketch in sharp focus, ignoring
the misty edge of mystery around –
all those shimmering shades between half-light
and laser blackness, the subtle shining spectrum
of the dark. But, for my mother's sake,
I would gainsay the mystery, would play
my part and stay, I thought, not understanding
that the very weight of gathered darkness
I denied and hid, would one day drag me
down, as then it did. Gratefully
I sank and melted into jetly shining
blackness; jewelled glistening; mirrors within
mirrors reflecting only deeper darkness,
into smooth embraces of subterranean
reaches to the hot black core. Now
I lived my truth. My true dark balancer
had waited for my consent of heart to draw me
down to his complexity of shadows.
He filled me with his knowledge, bound me by
the spell of all his secret understanding,
explored with me the folds and recesses
of wisdom. Let it be known that for myself
I never wanted to return at all

to the child's toys and picture books of earth.
Hades was my home. But human love
is strong, and the balance of our destiny
is tipped by more than our own wills. The cool
earth world is outward, separate, seen through lucid
windows at a distance, while these dark worlds
consist of touch and inner stimulation,
where I merge, dissolve and melt into all
and one. So if my story rings an echo
for you against the opening walls of halls
within, do not resist that shaded calling
but fall, give way, close your eyes and come.
Intent and smiling, empty-handed, dream
and sink and come beneath the earth, beneath
the waves, beneath the breath, and round the side
of sleeping death, as I did, into the indigo
obscurity of inner universes
lit by sudden flashes of inspired
stars. Come. Leave day alone. You deserve
to come... ... ... ...

# Commitment

*At one time in my life I faced inner choices about how far to commit myself spiritually. I struggled to balance my eagerness for inner mystical experiences with ordinary outer life on earth here and now. I also wanted to leave my intellectual options open and tried to avoid facing the faith I had come to have. These poems reflect that inner debate. I should like to emphasise, though, that they are not about being "born again" in the sense of evangelical Christianity. In fact I doubt the usefulness of organised religions of any kind. I simply found that I had shifted imperceptibly from an agnostic position to one of complete faith in my own idea of God and that I felt ready to acknowledge this inner change to myself.*

## Eighty Percent

I see myself as an eighty percent person.
I put the rest aside to propitiate caution.

I don't drain my glass with a reckless gulp.
I sip first to check the taste and evaluate.

I don't jump into the water. I dip my foot in,
recoil, try again later when the sun is warmer.

I don't like surprises, the unexpected visitor
ringing the doorbell, the sudden chance of a lifetime –

I prefer to think things over and get myself ready.
You can make such a fool of yourself without being careful.

I mistrust the dramatic conversion, the U-turn,
"the day my life changed", the re-birth.

I'm just mastering the predictability
of natural laws. I can't cope with miracles.

I prefer to sit at a desk and consider evidence.
I can't seem to rise to the big occasions.

I'm not prepared to discard my brain's scepticism.
It's served me well so far and kept my dignity.

So if you want to settle my life's account,
you'll have to put me down for eighty percent.

Perhaps you can count it as a deposit and take
the rest later, when I can't help it,

can't choose to stay and, weakened by the confusion
of that unpredictable transition

may, at last, perhaps, be drawn one hundred
percent, God, into your totality

## One Hundred Percent

I caught a faint scent of you
and suddenly remembered.
How could I think of giving less than all?

I had been like someone blind,
forgetting light, and then
the sun began to rise with slow assurance.

I rushed in frenzy round the house,
my poorly furnished mind,
the dingy corners of my meagre self-hood.

I tipped out drawers in my haste to offer
all the contents, shook out
my purse to extract the last gritty coin.

I grabbed at files of writing, diaries,
address books, credit cards,
and bank statements and threw them in a heap.

I dashed into doorways and surveyed rooms.
What else could I give, what else
did I possibly own of any worth to you?

The wardrobe of shabby clothes. The freezer
with its instant food.
The favourite picture, shelf of music tapes.

Now that I remembered, I could
hold nothing back. I longed
to fling it all down in front of you.

How could I have been so mean and with-holding,
so ungrateful, stiff and stand-offish?
How could I have been so completely dense and forgetful?

Now one whisper of that old
exhilaration and I am
scrambling and tripping over myself to run

into those arms, that light, that world
through the light; to dash out
without a coat, abandoning everything,

leaving the door wide open, the windows
unlatched, to throw myself
madly into that freshly recalled air,

that renewed savour of Spring.

## Resistance

How I resist love,
clinging to my sadness;
how I resist health,
clinging to my fears;
how I resist strength,
clinging to my weakness;
how I resist laughter,
clinging to my tears.

How I resist peace,
clinging to my conflicts;
how I resist help,
clinging to conceit;
how I resist truth,
clinging to my knowledge;
how I resist self-conquest,
clinging to defeat.

Help me despite myself
out of the labyrinth of blocks and bars
that the perverse complexities
of human arrogance and fears
endlessly construct against
what my whole self desires -
to open, trust, merge,
immerse myself in glowing water, air, fires -
whatever can describe the substance
that I truly am and all else is -
that which I insulate myself against
yet starve for; moping for lack of light
while screening off the sun, the moon, the stars -
absurd victor in self-destructive wars.

## Bargaining

If I give up
the wasting of my time,
watching television, reading
the papers, eating far too much,
enjoying the gossip, the witty remark
at another's expense,
the sharp flash of irritation,
the wide bellows of resentment
at my daily lot, my regret
at all the chances that I missed,
will you give them back to me again?

If I give up
my academic airs,
my small dips into culture – books,
music, theatre, ballet, art,
my tendency to teach and put
another right,
the carefully chosen pictures round
my room, my little mental hordes
of esoteric knowledge,
my intellectual complacency,
will you give them back to me again?

If I give up
that mixed bunch of qualities
I call my self, and all the roles
and fantasies I pose in
mentally and in my life;
if I give up
my easy ways, income, pension,
holidays, even home
and family, surely you don't
expect a blank cheque, no insurance?
You will in fact return them all again?

If I give up
hypothetically
these things that pad the rough edges
of living here on this tough planet,
that will be enough, I assume
from observation.
You really don't expect a genuine
amnesty, transfer of all
my weapons of survival, do you?
Nobody would take that kind of risk.
Of course you'll give them back to me again?

No.
I am God.
I know what's best for you.
I promise nothing, give no guarantees.
This is what faith is all about.
I may decide to keep the lot.
Yet you must really offer all you've got.

## Lying Low

I'm treading carefully around the house
trying not to be noticed. I avoid the floorboard
outside the airing cupboard, and sidle
round the bedroom door. They creak too readily.

Leaning breathlessly on the banister,
I step down the stairs in slow-motion
with a large stride to miss the fifth one down
that always squeaks gratingly.

I don't think there's anyone else in the house
but you can never be sure. I prefer to tiptoe
about, in case. I don't feel ready to face
a discussion, a parley, a decision. I'm lying low.

I wash up gingerly in the kitchen,
trying to avoid the clash of saucers.
I don't turn the radio on. If the doorbell rings
I freeze, out of the line of the hall window.

I jerk about in silence and caution
like a bird on the lawn alert for danger.
You never know when someone is watching
or lurking out in the garden, listening.

So much restraint and limitation,
but I like this place, I value my safety.
I prefer to hold on, rather than let in
the stranger, the wind, the terrible news.

This is my house, my familiar world.
I know it all. It's mine. Leave me alone.
Why should I open the door to risk
with its invitations and bright smiles?

## Filling the Gap

In the end I have to
let Love take control.
I never can be whole
by my own power alone.
I've tried the other ways.
After fifty years I own
my emptiness - a dried-up
stream, a sapless tree,
a ring without a stone.

I hoped to find my 'self',
some strong, distinctive dress
to cover and impress.
A self was what I willed
but never could achieve.
I did not mean to build
only an empty frame,
a hollow core, a gap,
a bottle to be filled.

Acting convincing roles
I was myself deluded
and foolishly concluded
that one at least of these
was really me, the one
I played with greatest ease
perhaps. With time I hoped
to prove the genuine art
among the forgeries.

But now I know that they
are all inventions, sheets
to cover mere conceits.
My house is bare. The light
is out. My senses register
without intention. My right
is only to give up
my rights, my paltry hopes,
surrender without a fight.

And then this other power
subsumes and quickens me
imperceptibly.
The dimmer switch moves round,
the bulb shines out. The low hum
swells into a sound.
A struggling of warm wings
within the cracking shell.
I am lost but found.

## The End of the Hunt

Perhaps I won't be noticed.
The last hope of the cornered fox
cowering from the hounds
with their devastating powers of smell.

Why would anyone finally want
that moment of annihilation,
the destruction of the ego?
I was mad to risk all this.

I thought I had embarked
on a love-affair, not a desperate pursuit
into a dark and silent thicket
in an empty plantation.

I thought to be chosen by God
was the ultimate honour,
a presentation at the palace,
a cause for congratulation.

But this is a lonely marathon,
returning exhausted to the starting-point,
throat and lungs cold
and sore from their gasping.

The whole of what I know
as self resists, fights on to the end,
will never hand itself in,
will never submit,

recoils shuddering from its pursuers,
although the cause is long lost
and I willed my own defeat
that moment in the fields

when I left the shade of the woods
and chose the open space,
paused in the centre of light
and invited, eyes glinting,

invited the inevitable chase.

## Over the Brink

I stepped over the brink.
only there was no brink.
I stepped again, thinking
I had failed to step
(my eyes were closed),
thinking the cliff-edge
and its dreadful drop
must have been further off.

The air solidified
into the crumbling chalk
I had just left.
It was a test, I thought.
To step just once or twice
could be from rashness,
desperation, fear's defiance.
I must step again.

A curious state of mind
now entered me –
elated emptiness
past fear, past caring,
past hope or struggle.
Consequences, self-analysis
were carried out to sea
on puffs of wind.

Again I stepped.
The earth still bore me up.
I found I could not fall.
Foundations still remained.
I could not move beyond support.
My life was underpinned.
Whether on air or ground
I was sustained.

Indeed I never stood
more firm than when I braced
myself and launched from land,
nor felt more anchored down
than when at last I took
that quiet measured pace
beyond earth's gravity
to a more solid place.

## Encounter

This is not what I was looking for.
I have tried to avoid this.
Kneeling at his feet I could cope with,
but not looking upwards,
not facing the blaze of his face's light.
I have tried not to meet his eyes with mine,
averted my glance,
kept back in my corner.
I don't like the limelight.
I prefer to admire from a distance.
It was not fear of him that held me back
from this encounter,
but dislike of self, unreadiness of heart,
and the certainty that to meet his eyes
is to lose control, to change.
Abstract absolutes - God, Creator, Love -
all were possible, were mind-approached.
Angels and guides I talked to like a perfect self
I could perhaps aspire to.
But this powerhouse of light
who must be related to as man
was different.
I could leave no part of me behind
in this invited confrontation.
He kept appearing in my path
gently, just to one side, waiting.
I scurried past.
I crouched in tears before the dazzle of his feet,
but then went on with head bowed down.
Tomorrow I would look at him
or when I was more worthy - never now -
until now - when I have looked,
exchanged a smile, been touched.
Now, at last, simply, a true meeting.
And in the gloomy dungeon void of me
his glow is entering entirely
every empty cell

## Alpha

This is how I was today
(Oh, words and their limitation):
A centre, pulsing outwards
as if, a stone dropped
into mirrored water, the waves
were spreading in perpetual
motion, renewing spirals
circling my meditation.

I was a state, a whole landmass
(Oh, the glow of it gone so soon)
without a beach or border,
unbounded, beyond illusion;
daringly unimprisoned,
throbbing with silent life,
a flow of unplayed music
free of form or tune.

A source, a spring, a well (feel
beyond the words' restriction),
the patch of sea first turned
by moon to generate
a tide. Pouring power,
today, for a moment, I was -
no words, no limitation-
Alpha, creating creation.

## Light

Brimming with light, awash with it,
I step about the house self-consciously
as if in a glowing space-suit. Brightness ripples
down to my fingertips, my toes, the end
of every hair. Minor electric waves
of it quiver through me. More and more
it pours and spills, refills, floods and overflows,
splashes about the floor.

How have I absorbed the sun
with moon and stars and all the manmade lamps
of earth? I no longer need to breathe it in,
but only out - out through my eyes, my breath,
my hands. Everything is strange to the touch
and unfamiliar, new to the sight, as if
experienced for the first time or the last,
simple, unique and right.

My hands savour surfaces with tenderness.
My eyes fire every object with sacredness.
My words are full of my heart's laughter and openness.
Weightless and strong as flame, I am drawn upwards,
dissolve outwards, every breath a tide
pulling the muddled world onto my beach
and letting it glisten out again, its drops
new-harmonised.

I surge with yearning, long to enfold
everything, catch everyone in light.
For this moment of being God, I need
a creation to embrace, inspire, ignite;
floating in this delicious welling spring,
dawning and beaming out my rising rays,
give me at least a world or two to love,
to spark, to set ablaze.

## What Next?

And afterwards what do you do?
After the holiday in the sun,
the evening at the ballet,
the complete absorption into the symphony,
the hour-long love-affair with creation,
what literally happens next?

Put the kettle on.
Bring the milk-bottles in.
Wipe the crumbs off the table.
Grey light in the kitchen.
The dog's blanket ought to be washed.

I need a hilltop to stride out on,
some moonlight over a river.
I want to walk on stage and sing.
An old Shakespearean actress
with mellow voice and grand gestures,
here I am in this kitchen drama.

I thought the light would fill my world
like a Spring day outdoors,
not throw the dust and grime into high relief.
I have seen both ends of a spectrum
and am helpless to unite them.

Perhaps it was all false,
yet another siren call of the jealous brain.
Perhaps the real light,
the real building-brick of the universe
is basic and non-separating,
does not manifest in visions,
will light up everything from within;
bring out the beauties in disorder,
the wonders of the process of decay.

But I have not known this.
Instead I struggle with lop-sidedness,
dusk punctuated by erratic day.

## Soon After

I don't feel well this morning.
May I have a day off from enlightenment?

I don't want to mirror divine light.
I prefer to get back under the duvet.

I like the visions and the healings,
the highs and the feel-good factors -

but surely not all the time?
Every thought, every hour, every day?

This morning I feel like wallowing back,
curling up with my old conditioning -

the comfortable prejudices, the old antagonisms,
the subtle pleasures of self-pity.

I can't summon up the energy
for all that effort of spiritual will-power.

I can't get the engine started.
My batteries are flat. There's no ignition.

Is there no sick leave? No excuses accepted
from now on ahead into appalling eternity?

## Overweight and Unfit

Now the hard work starts,
after that glorious vision of how I'd like to be.

I had no idea of the weight I was carrying,
and this is more arduous than a diet.

Not merely the denial of food
but careful selection of it at the thought-level.

Every feeling, every longing to be tested -
nutritious, positive, worth buying and serving?

I drag my limbs up the stairs,
my back aches, I feel worse than before.

I thought these grudges forgiven, forgotten,
but here they are still in my baggage.

And all my fear's protective padding -
pounds of weight on the bathroom scales.

I hoped to touch down like a feather,
be instantly empty, transparent, light.

But it looks like a long course of treatment
stretching ahead, a gruelling programme of denial,

a dose of spiritual weight-watchers.
I'm tempted to give up now before I start.

I'm not cut out for sainthood. Perhaps,
after all, I'll stick to being mortal.

## Let Me Keep It Quiet

Let me stand on the edge of the crowd.
Please don't call me in to the centre.

I like being the audience, but never the performer.
All those eyes and expectations.

I'm an observer by nature, a commentator, critic,
safe with my words at a desk of reason.

I dread being summoned, asked to come forward,
to walk down the aisle to the front of the meeting.

These public statements are so embarrassing.
How can I hope to keep my dignity?

This is all personal, intimate, secret.
I have the right to keep it private.

Dear God, I will sacrifice most things for you,
but not my control, don't take my control.

## Giving Birth Again

People talk of being born again. But this
is more like giving birth again at the age of fifty.

All the excitement and the mystery
of helping to incarnate some more divinity -

but also the nausea, the pain, the sleepless nights
and the prospect of total change to come.

I was just getting used to an easier life,
a bit more affluence, a comfortable routine.

I'm no longer sure I have the energy
for being turned inside out, jolted, shaken.

A short time off and I might just manage,
some time to think, get organised.

But day and night, so much to do, and youth
has not returned again miraculously.

I'm overwhelmed by pride and amazement
that this could have happened to someone like me -

and devastated with embarrassment
and the sudden weight of commitment.

Love is born to me and, love, I'm clinging
to you. I need you to see me through.

## Burnt Out

What happened to the exaltation,
the sense of floating down the stairs,
of being followed by a spotlight?

I burned out like a fire of paper.
A quick blaze and I was extinguished.
Now only the cold and a few grey fragments.

I thought I had been permanently promoted,
moved to the next floor,
but it was all a bitter show.

I see now that you were saying,
"This is your model. This is what to aim for.
Now get on with it yourself."

You showed the sweets and the big toys
to the child in me, then took them away.
How do I begin to get them for myself?

The morning after, my hair is lank,
my mouth tastes like greased vinegar,
my limbs are stiff and aching with remorse.

How was I taken in by such obvious glamour?
I should have stayed at home,
watched the television, gone early to bed.

I have been shaken up and thrown down again
for nothing but a dazzled memory,
a technicolour bubble, a stage effect.

I'd like to sink back again into my old ways.
I never sought for thrills and sensation.
I prefer my feet on the solid ground.

If it's a roller-coaster I'm offered,
I'll do without the views from the top,
when the only way down is to lose control.

And yet I know myself, my nature.
I need to hope, aim high, aspire.
No doubt I shall blunder back into that fire.

## Kindergarten

I may not like it
but I realise, of course,
that this is kindergarten stuff.

Daubing paints with a big brush,
glueing the primary-coloured shapes
haphazardly.

Cutting the biscuit-mix
with the teddy-bear cutter,
writing my alphabet with crayons

and taking them all back
proudly to mother
with a real sense of achievement.

The equipment is all set up
for my learning
and I stagger clumsily from piece to piece.

I count my successes in negatives.
No fighting, no crying, no tantrums,
no outright destruction.

I wasn't the one who broke the easel.
It wasn't me who pushed the boy
off the climbing frame.

I even helped to carry the milk for teacher
and tidy the chairs away.
I am really very good.

But that glimpse I had of light,
of love, was of an adult power
beyond obedience and simple rules.

It was the sunlight
of the massive world outside the village hall.
My pride goads me to run out there,

grow up, now, at once,
precociously,
and take on some real demands.

## How It Is

Morning and a sudden stillness.
Sunlight through the window rectangle.
It shifts like water on the turquoise carpet.
The carpet is in fact dog-haired
and, I notice, spattered with candle grease.
But this is earth and this is how it is
and still the sunlight and the silences.

The windowpane is streaked and mottled
and I can see outside a teatowel drying
on the rail. Yet the heightened glow
and quietness persist. Now in the kitchen
the washing machine begins its moist background
grinding; while I sit entranced, as if
preparing for some far orchestral sounding.

The milkman clatters on the porch
and the dog, woken from sleep, barks fiercely
for a moment from the shock. But still
in a space fluctuating with presences
I falter and adjust as if on entering
the damp dimness of an ancient church
from nettles, gravestones and bright light.

This is simply how it is -
having to keep the tension, hold the focus
between an immaterial translucent art
and the creative mess we form it from.
Dust and angels, stains and splendour,
decay and beauty, disturbance
yet an always-shimmering calm.

# Death

*I believe totally in a life after death (as well as reincarnation) and have always been fascinated by what exactly that might involve. In meditation I believe I have made brief excursions into that plane of existence and these have taken away any fear of dying. But, of course, a belief in life after death does not remove the pain of grief when we face the long separation from someone we love in this life.*

## The Baffling Dead

There is no vocabulary
for this, the no-language
of grief. I can reveal
what my brain thinks,
but where are words
for this vague pain I feel?

So the world says it for me,
in sudden glimpses
of old men everywhere,
stout in light raincoats
and flat caps,
with grey moustache and hair.

Behind me in a shop
I hear his sniff
or the timbre of his talk,
see someone else half-blind
bending, hesitating
with his careful walk.

And memory says it for me
in unexpected snapshots,
seconds of total recall.
I am sixteen.
He hunches out of the front
door as I stand in the hall.

Suddenly I am swaying
to school in a small seat
on his bike. I write
him a poem quickly
in bed before he comes
to say goodnight.

I lie in bed
and hear him laughing and arguing
in the room below.
I show him my report.
"Why not all A's?"
he wants to know.

He opens a can of beer or,
established in an armchair
like a rounded hill,
pours scorn at the News,
settled in his comforts,
searing in his views.

And all I can think is
"This was my father
and he is not here now."
No words for the strangeness of death
and the complex unwilled collage
the baffling dead endow.

## 11 June 1975

### (To Roger)

The coffin seemed to be made of lead.

The men were hoisting it from the car,
trying not to jerk or tip it,
panting with the exertion.

The sky glared, a blue sheet of stone.

We had talked about your father for three days,
but here was the visible weight of death.

All four of you were holding on to your mother,
gripping her hands, her elbows.
Her eyes and body strained forward.

She seemed about to raise her hands to help,
wanting to make things easier for him.

We and the crowd pressed back.
A moment engraved in marble.

A solid pressure loaded me down.
I wanted to run and cling to your arm.

As the men swayed into the church,
burdened with the heaviness of him,
her numb pain encased me in iron.

Could I in turn ever support this,
ever literally bear up,
staggering under the weight of your loss?

## Dying

Relief at the end of the day
to pull off those tight clothes
and stretch and sigh.

To gulp a long, cool glass
of water, parched after hours of work
under a quivering blue sky.

Sitting down to applause
flustered and thankful
after the dreaded speech,

or leaving the classroom after
a battering hour trying
but failing again to teach.

Pushing tiredly through the crowd
at the party, smoky and loud,
into silent midnight air.

Slamming the front door,
dumping the bags in the hall
and sinking down on the stair.

Easing off boots and rucksack
after the day's long trudge,
half-laughing at sudden respite.

Venturing from shelter, dazed
after the storm, shaking off drops,
face lifted to the light.

Wandering still bemused out
of the student exam, mind reeling
from pressure of time and of facts.

Climbing carefully down
the hospital steps to the car,
home to unwind and relax.

Eyes delighting to see
your lover surprisingly waiting,
quickening towards each other.

The wear and upheaval of labour past,
curious and tender, to stare
at your newborn child, a mother

at last.

## Crocuses

### (to Jean)

Driving by your house today I saw
your crocuses wide open to the sun
this second spring since you moved on through death.
I remember how you planted them, kneeling on
a rubber mat and sifting through the soil
meticulously. Your garden, house and life
were always neat and caringly controlled.

Of course, I know that you are still alive
somewhere, still yourself. I believe in this.
Often you are vivid to me in quiet
unexpected moments. Or I feel you
peering from behind me as I treat
someone ill or troubled. You will never
stop wanting to help and heal.

But though my underlying faith remains
latently unshaken, sometimes I falter
in my apprehension of that faith.
This world is solid, clear and sounding,
while my brain informs me you are dead,
transparent, silent and inhabiting
some doubtful dreamworld in my head.

Hard to believe in both worlds equally.
Consciousness inevitably focuses
within the body and the senses, not
the visionary mind. Yes, I believe
but not as much as in my sight
and hearing now, or in the smell of coffee
steaming here beside me as I write.

The purple crocuses that sunbathe in
the cold Spring light, throwing back their heads
beside the paving where I used to park
and let myself in at the end
when finally you couldn't leave your chair,
these flowers remain more real to me than you,
I must confess, until I join you there.

61

## To Jean, after her Death

Some people choose to die alone
and secretly.
They go into another room,
sit at their desks
or lie down on their beds
and do not move when called to have their lunch.

Some close their eyes in busy wards
rattling with cups,
invaded by officious trolleys,
until a nurse
in passing glances, pauses,
sharply tugs the floral curtains round.

One man I heard of
set off down a hillside running,
calling out "I'm flying"
only to collapse and fall to earth
mid-flight.

People whom neighbours have ignored
for years can find
an audience round their beds,
clutching awkward palms and tubes,
to see them off on this last trip from home.

While women who were known to be
the centre of their homes,
the pivot of their family's life,
decide to slip away sometimes
without a fuss and no one there.

I need to think, Jean, that you chose
a quiet parting too.
They say a nurse was with you.
We should all have been there,
crowds and queues of us
for you who thought of everyone
so well and caringly.

Take my goodbyes now, please.
Take my love.

I need them not to be too late.

## Terminal Illness

Could I believe that I was really sure
to die within a year?
Imagination gropes.
An abstract barrier
of doubt rather than fear.

My mind and my human shape already are
too separate to allow
parting. Images
of self glimpsed in a mirror
are of a stranger now,

so how could my mind be vulnerable
to its frame's disease? A tree
fall with its rotting branch?
Incomprehensible
this combined concept of me.

And if empathy from me to me fails now,
how could I tolerate
an identity condemned?
Project myself into slow
dimming, then neutral weight?

It's not so much that I'm afraid of death;
it just offends my reason -
my mind enclosing time
future and past, my breath
with its finite season.

I can't programme the thought; I'm only tuned
to forward strategy.
My brain rejects it. Half-
relieved I slip back down
the blank wall that hems me.

## Strange Addiction

Grief, that strange addiction
whetted by old reminders.
Its symptoms vary: anger,
guilt, self-pity, darkness,
the sense of the mortality
of all the world, the slipping
of one's own tenuous
gripping of reality.

Then, in the body, the twinges,
the spasms of pain, the exhaustion;
and all the time life's order
continuing, the cheerful voice,
the pleasant face of someone
a little distant from the self
maintaining, sustaining overhead
a thin and fragile surface, while chasms gape beneath.
Pot-holes, passages and black caves
wait to be mapped one day, later,
when that grasping concomitant
to loss is pacified and soothed.

Grief,
essential component of humanity
which all must undergo
in order to transcend; grapple with
to face with final equanimity
the last grief, for our own end

## An Easy Death

The house was quiet.
Distant traffic drone
intensified the stillness.
Motes of dust circled and hung.
The corner of the curtain idly flicked,
shaking a shadow on the counterpane.
Her hands lay heavy and immobile;
their clasp seemed curious beneath her stare.
Her mind was waiting motionless beside her,
unhurried and dispassionate.
The detailed background of her room,
ingrained in memory from living contact,
sank to a blur.
Only her hands remained in focus,
bent and gnarled like creamy softened twigs
or moulded pebbles worn to intricate design
by constant pressure of the busy sea.
She indulged herself in soothing passiveness,
her mind a vacant urn.
Restful relief of all her sense of self
spread up her like a sheet.

## A Death in the Family

There has been a death in the family.
Yet I make sure the washing's done.
The pile of shirts has to be ironed.
I put out the bottles and pay the milkman
while a part of myself has agonised and gone.

A bomb has burst at our very heart.
The empty crater's edge is sharp
and jagged. But while we shake in the dark
routine becomes a crucial art,
an external lotion for the inner hurt.

We still need meals and cups of tea
and homely food can help supply
the comfort needed. I go and buy
the household goods in the normal way,
push the trolley, queue at the checkout, carefully pay.

There has been a death in my family.
But I turn the television on
at the usual times, scan
blankly the news, the weather. When
the others leave for school and work, I just get on.

Part of me wants to take to my bed and stop.
But I make the beds and wind the clock up.
I may lean my head on the wall and weep,
but I keep an eye on the time. I sweep,
I dust. I am a mother and my role runs deep.

I am not in charge of these big events,
but still control the background; check
the library books; remember to take
the bread from the freezer; remember to meet
the youngest from school at 3.15; keep the garden neat.

There has been a death in the family,
a violence, a devastation,
but I continue the best I can.
Each tidy day is a battle won.
Everything is changed but everything goes on.

## Translation

They say that the dead will be translated
and I imagine the strange sensation
of dying and being born again in an unknown tongue;
the fainting breathlessness of slow erasure
as my strong verbs disappear,
the real declension of my nouns
and weakening of the old conjunctions
to those trifling attachments of articles
and prepositions needed no more.

Paragraphs, sentences,
even long pages of wordiness
I thought I had created melt in the high heat
of death; cliché, plagiarism and proverb
dissolve until the heap reduces
to a few persistent granules –
possessive pronouns: my, mine,
the personal pronoun: I, me. Then even
these evaporate into inky steam.

And at my side the curious words
form for my new persona,
strange linguistic clothing for whatever
core of me persists immutably
beyond translation, to try on cautiously
at first and then with confidence.
No doubt before too long in that
new habitat I shall convince myself
again I wrote them all myself.

## Landscape and Nature

*My holidays of choice have always been spent in the British
countryside, hill-walking and seeking out prehistoric sites. I
now live in Wales at the edge of the Cambrian Mountains so
I can indulge my love of wild places whenever I like. Like
Wordsworth, I actually believe that nature can be one of the
best and most direct spiritual teachers for human beings*

## Winter Countryside

I like this winter countryside.
It doesn't try to please.
Stark fences and the bare
wrought-iron
tracery of trees;

fields, scrawled on by tractors, olive,
khaki, mottled brown;
spiky smudges of hedgerows;
a scatter of gulls
like litter swirling down.

At the edge of forest, quavering smoke
from a damp, brushwood fire;
a corrugated roof;
a tangled copse
like a dump of barbed wire.

The sky, grey, ridged and solid
like the ground below
settles in and glares,
uncompromising
with its threats of snow.

As sharp as pencil marks still seen
through water-colour, the curving
lines of landscape stand out
fixed and hard,
timeless and unswerving.

Minimal and elegant
it looks me straight in the eyes,
like a model on a catwalk
in strange garb
who dares you to criticise.

Haughtily it says: You need not
comment, praise or flatter.
I simply am. Admire me
if you want.
To me it doesn't matter.

## Mountain

In the smoulder of crackling summer you drowse and sigh,
flicking off crashing boulders like pestering flies,
sweating the tarns off your shoulders.

In rain, you shiver, complaining.
You suck in all that is solid; and whine at the lines
of your chafing streambeds cutting their drains.

Behind my back, you inch - imperceptibly inch-
across valleys. Your fingers crack stone walls quietly,
hillocking hard-won fields in your sly track.

At night I hear you stir; you loom or recede
in gloom or glow of moon-clouds; turning over;
flexing stiff limbs; in sleep more deeply breathing.

At the distant aimed-for rim of the bare plateau
your glaring face suddenly shows and grimaces down
at my staring face below, till I dare not go.

As I saunter absent-mindedly, plunged in dream,
along a long leg, you bend it at the knee;
my balance swings like a compass and giddies me.

Carefree and confident, preparing to lope and run
down a rounded slope, I totter back; you have grown
since last time ribbed and thin.

I change with your moods; your petulant days
when, determinedly ugly, you sulk and brood; or when you smooth
and lift for pleasure your springy ways.

You challenge with paths crumbling to slithering scree
or ending in heather-tufts poised over wastes of debris;
you force me in corners, laugh and let me go free.

Retreating, jostled and baited, elated and sore
at the end of a day's round, time is tame before
I surge back for more.

## Silent at Llyn Teifi

Aluminium sky, black lake
and the cold air thick with grey rain.
The hills in pencilled lines,
unpolished woodcuts,
disappear in a bowl of creased ink.

Hoods up against the iced wind
we tramp in silence towards the dam.
The dog scuttles and slides
up and down the brackened banks,
a black drop splattered about by gales.

A sodden sheep tears up its mouthful
of wet grass and bolts away.
This is the right occupation for
a grim, blank day. Grim and blank ourselves
in the cloud and the mottled, sepia vacancy.

No one else has ventured out.
Self-contained we lean on the rusty railings
over the dam's concrete wall
and watch the wide expanse of dark liquid
combed and patterned by arbitrary gusts.

The weight of the water, the width
of the steel sky, the miles of moorland
stretching beyond the end of the road,
beyond the end of the track, where even
the sheep paths end in the final tussocks and bogs,

and ourselves like the litter at the dam wall,
knocked and buffeted by water and winds,
small and empty, not needing to speak
and strangely happy for once at knowing our place
in the wide order of things.

## Landscape and Time

Limbs of landscape
stretch and loll at ease
and over them the busy
forests crawl like ants.
Roads and hedges scrawl
casually and slow
lazily pastelled skies
billow above, nudged
by currents of calm.

Before I stopped
to gaze, I was a pent-up
powerhouse of will
and energy, buzzing
with imbalance. Now
I smile and dissolve. The sun's
ray on a patch of water
may glint blindingly
but settles to opaqueness.

I join the silence
and the size of hills,
their weight and tolerance.
I join the arbitrary
swinging of cloud shadows,
the draped folds of the fields,
the old stone walls launched
on a line of will, but petering
down to a crumbling standstill.

I am put in place
by the fractional stirring of hills,
the slight millennial shift
in the equilibrium
of valleys, and the huge
carelessness of the tides
of sky. Rooted as rock,
I brush off troublesome time
like a niggling fly.

## January Afternoon

Thin on the roofs and walls
from a blank grey sky
between bare hungry branches
straining high
the light snow falls.

It smears across the grass
and heaps carefully
in frozen teaspoonfuls
on bushes mournfully
huddling in a mass.

It teeters in icy piles
defying gravity
on narrow twigs,
abandons solidity
and slides off tiles.

Not the thick white
sugar purity
of Christmas cards,
but tight austerity,
almost but not quite.

Too bitter cold for snow
really to fall,
acid wind forbidding
more than a white scrawl
scribbled below.

The flakes shudder and toss
in the elbowing blast
across the bowed, colourless
January garden, past
hope, resigned to loss.

Indoors the strange light
pervades the gloom.
We wait by the fire
in the long afternoon
for the comfort of night.

## Red Kite

Red Kite sauntering up the valley
like a London VIP guest-of-honouring
at a country fete, the buzzard
a drab country cousin, the larks
and wheatears scuttling aside and lying low,
myself blatantly starstruck.

All elegance and perfection of winged line,
circling and cruising on,
it patronises the predictable forest,
the stream, the old-fashioned farm,
the sheep-untidy fields. Naturally
superior, self-consciously serene.

Plumage subtle but dominant,
the red-brown coat caught at an angle
in a snapshot of sunshine, offset
by a classic pattern of black and white.
The hooked curve of wingtips
matching the ruthless beak.

The black fighter planes that use the valley
for practice, imitating war
as they scream and blare overhead
in sudden blasts and invasions
hold none of the terror and easy power
of this silent forked intruder.

Squinting into the sun's glare
as the kite shoulders down over the hill,
and thinking of the dead sheep up there
that disappear entirely within days,
I linger mesmerised, like a
shadowed vole or a mountain hare.

## Holy Wells

It is not so much their use for healing,
nor their antiquarian appeal;
nor the valuable source of pure water
for drinking, springing from the ground year
after year since first their flow was found.

Certainly their sacredness soaks
the whole moist air around like any shrine
and sobers the mind with sense beyond the mind.
A numinous stimulation, almost addictive.
These are justifications of a kind

for the long journeys and the tedious time
spent searching fields and culverts, map in hand,
feeling a fool, unwilling companions striving
for patience, until one finds some over-grown
brown-watered, stone-edged, undistinguished pool.

But the real magnetic pull of them -
ancient and instinctual - remains
the moment standing before an orifice
of earth and sensing the rising flood
powering up the hidden paths and lanes

to the brain's surface and breaking into air
and thought, spilling out into the seen
and tangible from the running chaos
of the liquid dark, that earth pumps
through her capillaries and veins.

I watch it over and over, bubbling, trickling,
filling, and am consoled by the infinity
of flow and by the assurance of the hidden
watertable constantly respread,
richly refilled below.

## Dawn in the Nunnery Chapel on Iona

Standing inside the ruined chapel,
my back against the western wall,
I speculated how the light might fall
at different seasons on the nuns
who, dawn by dawn and year by year,
knelt and sang and mused and pondered here.

As the morning sun swung over Mull,
long ladders of light, leaning
through windows and the screening
sky, would have stretched and reached
upwards and westwards in their angled flight.

The island seems indeed to float on light -
not dry and shaking with meandering dust,
but liquescent, swishing, speeding,
continuously inrushing and receding,
turquoise, brushed with amethyst and pearl.
It has colour-washed the stones, and ground
its spectrum back to a fine compound
of white sand on the scalloped frame of the shores.

Round their chapel the nuns would also gaze
in shade, or blink in dazzling blaze
at carved corbels of moon and sun and stars,
and an angel, met perhaps in dreams
or glimpsed within those straight streams
of lustre that daily soaked them in sacredness,
those bright buttresses of air
that underpinned their house of prayer.

Light was their sacrament. They led their lives in it,
immersed, transformed within its glow
until it made them eager to forgo
the opaqueness of their peaty earth and wade
out through its gleaming track
across invisible oceans back
beyond the force of tides to its silent source.

## Linhope Spout

Grey February. Over Linhope Spout
a dull muzzle of mist. Thirty feet
of burn-brown, frothing and steaming, white
and pounding water in a violent jet
scours at unyielding rock with all its channelled weight.

Smears of grass streak and drip. A bowed
tree grovels, stretching a clawed
branch down towards the force, over the cold
of running rock, the cold of moss and mud
by ages of drumming downfall smashed and mauled.

The fog will not give or clear.
No one else comes. We just stand and stare
and stand. There is nothing to say
before this pent-up thrust of bursting power
exulting alone, indifferently, all day, all year.

There is nothing at all to say.
Words, mind, time are swirled away,
drowned by din and undiminishing downpour.
Only our flesh and hungers are felt above the roar,
relentless as the rock, cold as the brown spray.

## History and Place

It is not so much this crumbling earth,
the flaking slate of rocks,
the grey pebbledash roughening the house walls
in the cold sunlight;
it is not literally these I love,
but what has gathered in the air beyond them –
accretion of experience and feelings
clinging like moss and lichen to the valley,
the sudden pleasures of the past
left in pools of lightness,
grief, and anger in patches of coldness,
the lingering worship of whatever gods.

It is not so much the scraping of branches
in the ash-tree growing in the ruined barn
but the tremors of old conflicts still vibrating;
tintabulations of family quarrels
still rubbing in hazy layers
around the homestead;
old harmonies still holding
the stone walls close together.
The bond between man and the soil
remains from centuries of sowing, tilling, reaping,
though the shepherd only visits now
from time to time from down towards the town.

It is not the call of governments
or stirring of the orators
that makes a love of place and country.
It is the pull of the past in corners of quietness,
the sense of continuity,
not in a long line dimming back
into millennia, but heaped
in frothy invisible layers in one spot,
enriching it with memory,
history's overtone chanting, brimming
with levels of harmonics, that resonate
into the body beyond the logic of tune.

# Bats

Between dusk and blind night
they dart in the dark;
before curtains are drawn
and evening lights turned on,
they swoop and accelerate
from my house wall
in ecstatic aerobatics.

As the town stills down and moves
inwards to the warmth of hearths,
they fling and sling themselves
like black fireworks against
the blackness. The silent erratic
explosions of their silhouettes
can be missed by a blink.

Boomerangs of the borders
of light and dark, of life
and sleep, half-way creatures,
almost birds, launched
in speeded-up regattas
of disorder, they swoop and sail,
a volley of arbitrary arrows.

I hold myself tense
and sensitised, hardly
breathe, to hear their wing-rush,
to glimpse their unpredictable
directioning, the hurl
and flick of them out
of the ivy's vertical forest.

Gradually the thickening air
out-blackens their rocketings,
and for the toss of a moment
my own wayward bursts
of thought also subside
into the swelling sentient
density of dark.

## Summer Grasses

Outside the kitchen door is a bank
of stones and wildness, once a rockery,
but now encroached by hill and moor.
Branching sorrel
and foxgloves sway
above bracken.
Nettles give way
to sturdy mint.
Solid mottled brown
of plantain heads
bow up and down.
But mostly now
as August passes
it holds a tiptoe
dance of grasses.
Teetering further and
further upwards they dare
to stretch impossibly
from earth to air.
In complicated
rearrangement
their stems regroup
in constant interchangement,
swishing like horses' tails
at the teasing flies.
Profligate plumage
of the mountain sides;
thousands of small straw feathers;
blowing banners
braving all weathers;
nodding, bending,
held aloft,
standards of sunlight
grainy and soft.
Twitching, revolving
to different times,
they lean across
and intertwine.

Grasses like spiders' webs,
diaphanous and bright
as summer snowflakes,
catch dew and light.
Clustered seedtops
of dried honey interlink
with others faintly
tinged with pink.
The permutations
of their delicate display
and patterning
confound me every day
as I shake the breadcrumbs from the board,
throw out the tealeaves, wring the cloth
or merely gaze – blurred, lulled, amazed.

## Clogwyn Du'r Arddu, Snowdon

For all this I long to be alone,
on my own with the stinging cloud of snow,
no one leaning against me but the wind.

Ahead, Clogwyn's black sliding grooves
and sheer sides of pyramid rock compress
their powdered boulders down to the steel below.

I want it to myself, the cloud sifting
over it fistfuls of snow, then drifting between,
smothering the tough unbowed hardness over again.

And back I want to hunch alone, across
the scrunching tufty waste, and slog on down the track
oblivious as the blizzard to all but what I must.

To see alone, through shifting wells of cloud,
the weight of hills keel over and away
or, miles below, Llyn Padarn gaping clear.

I crave today to be aware of the sharp
thrill of loneliness, that bare sense of self
in the centre of acres of air.

For this is no sport nor mere view to be shared.
The place, the time, myself deeply combine in a quick
pull of fusion, that can only ever be mine.

# Sky and Stones

*In the second part of my life I became fascinated by the prehistoric monuments ruined and largely disregarded across the moors and hills. This led me to the only obvious explanation for their locations – their link with the sky. I studied archaeology and later did a further degree in ancient astronomy and astrology. These poems reflect some of my experiences as an amateur archaeoastronomer.*

## Lunar Standstill November 2005

Everything blotted out including
skyline and the huge quartz stone
aimed for at the field's edges.
Falling over the hard ridges
of furrows, in a blind passage,
with holes and tussocks tackling
my ankles in a constant scrummage.

Compass, map, unstopping watch
useless without the torch
I forgot. And the moon won't wait.
Stumbling about in the dark
in a headlong mindless state.
After all the sums and theories
now I'm going to be late.

A faint glow roughly
where I expect, landscape
shadowed rather than black. The loom
of a dimmed lantern arriving soon.
Frantic steps more manic.
Breathing pumped by panic.
And then, together, stone and moon.

Blinking down, the moon tips
its head over the counterpane
of hills, starts to waken,
and stir in silence, to unchain
itself from its marked place,
enacting the old patterns again
with impassive face.

It is probably where
I calculated. I no longer know.
Angles and azimuths dazzle
away in the stately, slow
amplification of light,
the rising roundness of glow
and more than the maths is right.

## Waiting for the Moon

Miscalculation. Knew the time of sunset
but assumed the eastern skyline
opposite was lower than it is
to observe the rising of full moon.
It must come soon.

Too early now. Impatient.
Pacing across the rough field
swiping at thistles. Meal cooking in oven.
Can't make the family wait.
Can't be late.

My own fault. Too hasty. Life
pulling in all directions.
Want to be here, should be there.
Breathless from rushing up the slope too fast
in case the rise had passed.

This unhurried certainty
this abstract high sailing
on the broad smooth current
of the ecliptic, never late,
can irritate.

Total predictability,
inflexible, while people
scuttle about and compromise
trying to do too much,
losing touch.

Nothing I can do. Just sit down,
calm down, contemplate,
until that great white face lifts
slowly up over the hill
as and when it will.

## Winter Solstice Sunrise

Stamping and flailing arms
in midwinter coldness,
we watch the sky flicker and lighten
with rising intensity;

wait so long we are almost surprised
when over the hill's brink
floats the golden balloon,
almost transparent.

We stare up, dip down, stand again,
align both stone and sun,
its glare and power blinding
as it swells.

We jump about dazzled,
take our photographs, hug
one another, cannot respond
to the moment's momentum.

Rolling and wheeling
along the hilltop the huge orb
takes off on its shortest flight
low round the sky to the night.

And afterwards, stumbling
downhill, the golden round
transparency imposes itself
on every muddy flank

and rivuleted surface
of the winter valley, on gateway mud,
on tired and sodden fronds of bracken,
broken clumps of reed,

on ruined barn and crumbling wall,
across the lens of eye and mind
a filter of gold on our way
back to the warmth.

## Winter Solstice Sunrise, Pontrhydfendigaid

Only at one heaped tangle
of massive boulders
does the drapery of hills above
pull itself to a right angle.

A neat half-square,
side and base composed
of the nearby hill and the one
beyond, up in the air.

Here I am alone in the cold,
leaning against the dampness
of rock and waiting
for the yearly drama to unfold.

Cars pass on the road,
children shout in the school
playground, unaware
of this dramatic episode,

this annual combination
of local scenery with time
when the sun reaches its
furthest southern station.

On the black ledge
of the skyline the golden disc
begins to glare, lifting up
over the solid edge –

as it has from this spot
over and over for
thousands of years,
noticed or not.

It starts to climb
away from the cold land,
in a dazzling silent show,
a spectacular mime

put on for me alone,
an unworthy observer,
small and inadequate
by the patient stone.

## Landscape Art

The landscape was their palette, easel,
final work of art, if art expresses
self in the context of the universe.
One megalith, perfectly placed, compresses '
a total statement of knowledge handed down
and understood - seasons and cycles of sky
where they touch a landscape's local rim.
Stasis of stone brought to life by the sun or the moon.
A photograph waiting its time to transform
from still life and sleep into moving film.
But the rest of the countryside canvas left alone.
No need to decorate nature overmuch.
Minimal art, just getting the job done,
understatement with a strong, sure touch


## No Moon

On the nights before the first crescent manifests
as the backcloth dims after sunset,
or on the nights when clouds block the white lamp,
however round,

and the scatter of stars offer no glimmer,
I am supposed to be disappointed.
But going outside to check the state of the sky
I can walk into blackness,

the total privacy of night, when
my face is unseen and I can bury it
yet breathe in the soft pillow of darkness
smoothing my cheeks.

Then there is only that self which is me
invisibly present in the universe
scanning through blind eyes for signs
of the physical

and hoping not to find them.

## Song of the Stonehenge Astronomer

Even my dreams are full
of the rich precision of eternal number,
sun and moon bouncing slowly
off the earth's edge in perfect parabolas.
I ignore the frost on the grass,
the high larks in standstill wavering,
the broken bracken of autumn.
People come and go
like mice among the uprights of a barn.
My eyes are directed to the universe,
my body tense with expectancy
at the base of the moment's angle.

Hub of the wheel of the world,
centre point of the compass of time,
I swing magnetically to the pull of the light.
Massive and oblate, the blazing orb
heaves heavily from the ground
between the towering slabs of shadow
with perfect timing in its moving pattern.
Vibrating light in geometric line
joins me direct to the dazzling centre;
sun and human linked, earth and heaven
bonded in mathematical union.
Once again life is preserved in order.

From the stone ring of record
and prediction I observe it all -
solstice and equinox and quarter day
marked by the resolute clock of light
that holds in check the year;
and the changing moon, slimming and swelling,
soaring high or swooping low
in a dipping, rising ritual
that lasts a generation;
flowering curves and concentric sweeping
gestures drawn in white and gold
against the blue and black.

This is my duty and my being,
my occupation and my aspiration.
Human life seems paltry and disordered
with its aimlessness and quick decay.
Here I hope to die, at the centre
of eternity, my spirit in its proper place,
my aged body borne away
far outside the purity of the circle
which will hold true for ever,
steady watchtower of the great rotations,
fulcrum of universal balance,
infinite keeper of time among the stars.

## Mid-Winter

I know what it's like to feel the grip of winter,
the frost clamping deep into my ground;
the unlifting pressure of relentless cold
that binds me helplessly in heaviness;
the aching immobility of waiting, waiting,
glacier emotions heaving and creaking blindly
with painful strain.

I know what it's like to feel the paralysis,
the injected ice numbing the secret channels
of my senses. No growth. No movement.
No murmur of possibility and change.
The imprisonment of the body chaining the spirit.
Sun a distant dream and vague hypothesis
greyed out and stupefied.

The moment of the solstice turns beyond
our hope and our control; that moment
of relief when, stretched to its furthest limit
along the horizon of endurance, the sun
imperceptibly draws back and soothes and softens,
initiating the flow and melting, the stirring,
starting the trickle, the greening, the glow.

## Then and Now

What difference do a few millennia make
to the lungs, pumping to persevere,
to the radiation of blood, reddening the face,
to the breath breaking like waves in the ear
as we climb, panting and hunched in a daze
towards sky? Then as now the laughter would disappear
for the final push to the peak, under the weight
of poles and provisions and layers of clothes, to wait
for the moon, unfussy and smooth, who will never be late,
who will always be cool and whose patterns of ebb and of flow
can be known in advance but are never within our control.
Her light softens a patch of horizon and over the brow
she appears. We scramble and clamour, each with a pole,
to line up the moment, whichever millennium, now.


## Full Moon

Trying to write a poem
about my half-defined ideas,
unformulated feelings
the moon, golden and metal-edged,
totally round, unnatural
and hard as a newly-minted coin
sheening with electric brilliance
on a night-blue table-cloth,
rises inexorably behind my shoulder,
saying nothing,
as it drills its way through my windowpane.

Symbol today only of the material.
Classic demonstration of total objectivity.
Pure geometry.
Its reality bores through my bone.
Dreams, thoughts, life
merge and dissipate translucently
before this fact, this presence,
this actuality that dominates from far.
For I may make and recreate myself,
but some things simply are.

## Sunset at the Megaliths

In touch
with the touch of the sun
lowering steadily down
on the black horizon of earth, to tie
these stones in an angular line to the sky.

In sight
for once of the hidden orbit of earth
and the clock's rotation,
gliding me backwards away
from the light of the darkening day.

In tune
with the people who, aeons and eras ago,
located this link-point of planet
and time, and to make it perpetually known
marked it with heavings of stone.

In place
to observe that the tilt of the earth
has changed and the lower limb of the sun
and its final flash have shifted to show
more than the time of the year in the last of their glow.

In line
for a lingering moment with past
and with present, the muted hills here
and the universe endless and blue -
while the first stars flick into view.

## Out of Touch

Under loft timbers and slates
in my book-lined room
I am out of touch
with the sun's parade
and the dippings of the moon.

Contact has been lost between
the universe and me.
I have buried my head,
blind to the sun's beam
and the moon's diversity.

My key is lost to the map
of the sky. I can't predict
where the sun might roll
around the zodiac
or where the stars are fixed.

It is a language once known
but forgotten, the changed street
of a town I knew
but am lost in now, a tome
of knowledge for an illiterate.

I am bereaved of my family,
the sense of where I am
in time and space,
of where I belong under the canopy
of changing air; orphaned.

Out of harmony and phase
from the beat of moon and sun
but restless to relearn,
hungry to return my gaze
where order issues from.

## Maen Gwyn

My thoughts fingered out
into the winter darkness
round the lightless house –
the deeper silhouettes of trees
against the greyer grass;
the black block of the road
that rises like a wall
on these moonless nights;
the absence of horizons;
and the fields humped
under blanketing counterpanes,
their senses closed
in sleep-unconsciousness.

But one light shone
and could not be put out.
As if lit from within
by a glow of grey-silver,
the white quartz stone
on the mound along the lane
would not be dimmed.
It throbbed silently
in my head, like a church
with the candles left forgotten
all the night, flickering
to the music it had known
and the echoing prayers.

# Love and Marriage

*I have been married to the same remarkable man for over forty years and his loving support and tolerant companionship have been central to my life. We have two children, now adult, and a grandson.*

## Domestic Incident

Enthusing earnestly in the kitchen
on poetry and the ideal state,
brandishing pet resentments with my wooden spoon,
importantly convinced of what is right;
ridiculously poking the simmering pan,
I become aware of too much quiet
in you, my audience, and turn
to find you round the corner of my sight
laughing at me silently. Indignation
surges a moment, but fails. The words deflate.
I'm forced to share that grin.


## To Roger

The house is full of empty spaces
where you ought to be.
No clattering down the stair,
no one to turn the radio on loud,
no one competing for this chair;
the bathroom's always free.
I miss the daily instalments
of your office gossip,
your sweeping forcefulness,
your insecurity.
The way you say splendid goodbyes
and then return
for something left behind.
Your flourishes,
your warm and loyal heart,
your sudden rigorousness of mind.
Hurry home.
I miss your words, your touch;
no other voice or hand will do.
The house is full of emptiness and echoes.
It needs you.

## Married Love

I don't wear love any longer, putting
it on with delight in the mornings,
slightly self-conscious of it during the day.
Now it's as much a part of me as the creases
around my eyes, the few hairs growing grey.
There's little room for tender proud display
now that we overlap; each is too much the other
to wonder at the points at which we join.
We share unthinkingly our breath and bodies;
our world is seen through four eyes now.
I hum around the house that's neutral as
our love, untidy with valued memories,
neither a source of pride nor shame, but just
our place. Shelter, warmth, quiet, space.

## Marriage

Not our whole will
        can make a total fusion,
superimpose and unify
        our complementing mysteries.
Unseeable and separate we remain –
        our two identities
felt only, through a darkness.
        Closeness can bring illusion
from time to time of oneness
        (while it destroys perspective)
but, shifting closer still,
        I suddenly slip free,
grope to grip you for security
        and find that grasps are tentative
with this blurred vision –
        your self, despite your will
and mine, eluding me.
        Impelled by love and loneliness,
the desperate instincts of the mind
        move us towards a harmony
we struggle to maintain;
        alert to keep equal our balance,
in endless, eager sequence
        we test, retract and modify,
touch, link, release again,
        hopefully edging on to find
the other – hopelessly blind.

## Resonance

To be with you is to chant with you.
You set me ringing like glass,
chiming in rhyme with you.

Across the room, the taut strings
of my open senses hum in unison with you.

Deep within my murmuring frame
each mellowing organ fills and swells,
following in time to you,
vibrating with the note of you,
combining with the fine tune of you.

Our voices bell like fluting overtones
above melodious silent echoing billows
flowing and counter-flowing
below us, between us.

The mute volume of our harmony
magnetises into musical design with us
the separate sounds of background birdsong,
sudden surges of chatter,
traffic drum and mumble.

The shaking air shines into patterns with us.
The furniture, the books, the walls
shimmer and fall into glimmering resonance.

Together we merge into a mantra,
irresistibly intoning
the whole roll of the earth through the space of our breath.

From two alone we unite into one,
from one attuning into entirety.

## Belong Only to Love

Belong only to love,
not to me.
Be caressed
but not possessed,
be free.

Love's flow and overflow
pour constantly.
All I convey,
all I relay
springs not from me.

Love is its own source
and its own sea,
cannot be owned,
only loaned,
is always free.

Love gives, not to receive
but to make grow.
Love inspires,
creates desires
to stretch and go.

Belong only to love,
not to me
and love's embrace
will give you space,
will set you free.

## This Lovely Desire

This lovely desire,
soak-softening my limbs,
touching and fronding my skin,
sounding my sensibilities,
melts me towards you,
towards your warm-hungry hands
and melts me smilingly towards all life.

The nestling sheet of the sky
is so blue-enveloping.
The lifting, whispered breathing of the wind
smooths and gentles by me
like the back of your hand along mine;
like your breath, very light,
quick and restrained against my brow.

How warm and beautiful life is,
how ardent the need to create,
the need to give, to reach out,
to share reciprocally,
to play these delicate powerful roles,
controlling urgency,
savouring subtlety.

We sway like the long grasses in the garden;
dart out and retract like the luminous dragonfly;
building, busying like ants on their anthill,
compelled by the urge of creation and increase.

Yes, this lovely desire,
blurring me outwards,
misting the borders of self and self,
compels me joyfully, through you,
into all the soft, hard, swelling
planet-power and pulse of amazing earth

## Together at Home

My head's a cloudless sky.
Your old 78s drift and drone
out through the honeysuckle to where I sink and glow
in a sun halo of pure sensation.

Powder scent of grass.
The cat nuzzles and arches on the warm stones.
The pond drinks and swells from the garden hose.
A breeze sighs and drowses off again.

Hair brushes my lips.
I am malleable, melting deep in my heavy bones.
Time's a mere throb of the blood on my wrist.
I press my smoothness gently against my clothes.

Indoors you hum
vaguely and clatter glasses, like mine your face
a blur. Sensitised more deeply, still one,
our minds have not yet slipped back into place.

Don't come yet,
stirring the haze, with the drinks and tender banter.
My smiles are curling round and around me. Wait,
suspend the present a little longer.

## Basic Elements

I don't speak of my relationship
with earth. I throw
my weight on it incautiously.
Tough and essential, slowly, its wordless energy
rides me round through space,
growing my life,
inseparable from what it means to be.

Or air. It simply starts my blood off.
It's breathing through me now
no will involved, no soft words spoken.
I see the whole world through it
unaware, until it concentrates
into a sudden gale, or stays so still
the quiet lifts my head and makes me stare.

There's no wooing between myself and water.
I'm thirsty and I drink. Look
how I can't hold it, yet it's calmly here
always. Unthinkingly my sheer
need takes it for granted.
Receding, surging, the buoyant sea
remains a neutral fact whose currents carry me.

So what words serve to link myself
and this live element you are,
this universe I could not speculate beyond?
When I start to think, the confidence
of my reliance draws me,
like fire, with wary wonder
and the water, air and earth of my warm
body merge in a steady flame.

## Sharing Sleep

I smile at the cat's bliss,
stretched snug on my still lap,
a comforted warming weight,
claws flexing a little, sighs swelling
as the coals settle and shift
late in the quiet hearth
and I, gently, contort to write;
vulnerable, he breathes security
from the warmth
of his trusting body next to me.

And how much more, at ease
in the dim and shared sinking
of our bed, next to your heat
and heavy hollows, your turns
and murmurs, despite the night's
rustles and scuffles, I feel a relaxed
simple languor, the welling
certitude of sleep, serene safety
from the warmth
of your loved body next to me.

## When You're Away

When you're away
the shutter closes
dust sheets conceal
the fire crumbles
breath pauses

the chimes delay
the minutes saunter
dimly I wait
for you at last
at last
to enter

When you are late
I will not be a fool,
but deny, repress and question
the debilitating tension
that only threatens now with sickly tick
but soon may strike.
I grip and clench and tighten.
I make a conscious effort not to think
yet think -
the thought-crevasses can so subtly
gape and frighten.
The most unstable point is on the brink.
Imagination irritates and flares,
enters and overwhelms me unawares.
But though in truth appalled
I will not be a fool
I will control, control.

When you arrive
the air relaxes, windows open,
clocks resume a reassuring beat,
the daily volume is again turned on.
Ideas, words and laughter rush together,
the black and white are coloured in.
Our separate lives, unhurriedly,
reach out and fuse, back into one.

## Silences

I am aware of silences within you,
gaps of stillness
like skies between the branches of a wood.
Could words or touch in some way
link those silences of yours with mine,
unblock and open passageways
from emptiness to emptiness,
together we could make a space
to hold a universe -
neither dark nor light
but neutral, still
and waiting
till galaxies should spark
and suns and moons ignite.

## Fusion

When I lie back
within a world of feeling dark
and let my body meld and melt
and mould with yours;
when I am planted,
growing, blooming at your touch
and, deep into deeper shades
of darker darkness,
in my inmost self receive
your love and longing,
and we share the pulsing
and momentum of the life force
making oceans, rocks and molten streams;
when I am only sensibility
and nerve, yet also mingling
with the tolerance and ease of earth,
petalling open, sepals folding back,
stamens delicate and aching
with the power of sunlight joy

then too can come a spark
of inner bliss, samadhi of the soul,
fusion beyond the flesh
where you and I, the elements
and every living thing
whirl giddily as one.

## Liquefaction

And so we flow
in the streambed of each other -
an impossibility!

How winding and complex you are,
so many corners and overhangs to spread into;
so many twists and overflows and tributary rivulets.

How can the directness of passion
adapt itself to such newfound fallings,
blocks of boulders,
the eddying round pebbled beaches
and sudden silent pools?

Breathlessly I long for water's flexibility,
its sinuous reaching,
its instinctive levelling;

long to be as warm and limpid for you
as sunlit shallows,
while still as darkly strange and other
as deeply shadowed fern-hung hollows.

Mind set aside on the bank,
I can only be carried
by and with my liquefaction,
by the melting silken threading of it;

only sense out and down and in and through,
relying on the open waiting channel of you,
propelled by my own weight
and the universal law that draws me on -

love's gravity,
that causes me always to waterfall down
towards you.

# Home and Family

*Being part of a generation of women who normally left their careers to bring up their children, I have spent a lot of time in my own home and love the concept of a place and a group of people providing a supportive base from which to approach the world. I am no housewife but have loved being a mother.*

## Home

Pause, grope with the key,
and shoulder the sticking door,
while the cat creakingly stretches
and comes for his fuss.
Drop the bag, the coat, the books
on the hall floor and sink
in the chosen clutter that represents us.

Kick off the day with the shoes,
uncurl the toes, soften the face.
Now to breathe, increase, expand -
to dance a ridiculous dance,
destroy the pose
and pretensions of dignified hours,
grow younger and

later, each side of the fire,
the cat between,
three clocks ticking different times,
smile and ignore
the mess and the washing-up
(silence is clean through the pipe-smoke;
unmoulded identity more

precious than order). Soon we'll lie
warm in the night while the weather
rustles outside the window
and, without speaking, we'll share the stillness,
knowing that these familiar, trite,
amazing moments are to be savoured,
forgetting tomorrow.

## Perfection

This is perfection now -
the dear dust on the windowsill;
the smears across the kitchen window pane
that form patterns in sunlight
like faults and filigrees that grow
within a crystal; the rampant honeysuckle
that will imminently fill
the frame, its untrimmed stems twisting,
entwining, swaying until
they spill out in thrilling vertigo
over the garden a floor below.

The tulips, picked a week ago,
also are perfection. They burn like slow
fire in their water. Their flexing
crimson petals stretch to dropping point,
uninhibited and open wide to life.
They flare and flow. Yet were perfection too
when closed and secretive and new,
trembling at the point of close control.
Moment by moment, angle by angle,
perfection can rearrange
itself, can grow and change.

Because I love this place -
the children's pictures on the wall, askew,
the cat's old plastic dish,
the fading posters - every part
combines harmoniously for me like art.
It is perfection's law
that loving eyes embrace
a scene and draw haphazard details
into the balance of beauty -
wholly perfect with grace
the disparate features of a much-loved face.

## Parenthood

Standing at the kitchen window
I watch her setting off across the lawn
over the paving stones,
then turn with a hop under the climbing frame,
to wave and laugh at me.
The regular morning ritual.
Nine years old, fair hair untidy in the wind,
school skirt already twisted askew, shoelace
undone, rucksack heavy on her back
with the choice of books to fill the day's gaps.
She would leave for school earlier if I let her.
She shouts a password and I have a struggle
to recall the right reply. Using both hands
she manages the latch and disappears
at last, still grinning at me, through the gate.
Pride, love and amusement jostle in me
as I turn back to the littered kitchen –
a clench of pain, too, deep inside
at all the valiant vulnerability
which I must let her keep. For loving her
is giving her the chance to grow, the risk
of freedom, endlessly giving back herself.
Indeed at the heart of the art of parenthood
this constant act lies tenderly in wait –
to smile and wave goodbye cheerfully
as your children disappear beyond your gate.

## Artemis

### (Harriet)

Up at first light, even in wind and rain,
to catch the old Welsh pony (as independent
and tough as she is), she rides out scattering
sheep and birds, before parents complain
about where she's going or insist she wears her hat
as, over the rough ground, she gallops ecstatically
clutching a buzzard's feather she has just found.

Slim, supple and terrifyingly fit,
in the dammed-up pool in the mountain stream,
cold and exultant, brown with peat, she will swim
naked almost any day between Easter and autumn.
Sometimes she is a Red Indian straight from her tepee,
and sometimes will writhe and slip in the icy water
being an otter, wild, untameable and lithe.

She is fiercely argumentative and sharp
as her sheath-knife on almost any subject,
especially with her brother, whom she also
adores. Yet is patient for hours with puppies
and young children. She wants sympathy for her scrapes
and bruises, but angrily pushes you away
if you strike the wrong note in what you say.

Statuesque, across the fields on the skyline
with her blanket wrapped round her and her long hair
blowing, she might be a Celtic princess or
a red kite about to launch into air.
In the house, she shrugs carelessly
over frequent breakage, loss or spill.
Except when gripped by a book she is never still.

Yet is so wise a goddess in understanding;
so intense for peace and fervent to do good.
Ancient at eleven, no wonder she gets
impatient with adults who should know better.
No one society or culture clutters her.
Taut as a bent bow, she can outvie
in ferocious purity the towering sky.

114

## When You Left

(To Tom)

When you left, the light changed.
I was not prepared for it. I planned
to be busy and practical, but a strange
sky loomed over, and snow settled with a bland
expressionlessness, padding and wadding the gloom,
and the odd, cold light diffused into every room.

I sat dolefully by the window -
just as I intended not to do.
The sky sagged and dragged with its weight of snow.
The garden laurels were numbed and frozen through;
with dismal fortitude they drooped and shifted
as down through cellular silence the grey light sifted.

Self-indulgence of that kind
I wanted to avoid. The torn sensation,
the inner shakiness, I did not mind
until that light disclosed my dislocation,
revealed my feeble acquiescence
in that curious clarity of luminescence.

It would have happened anyway,
that alteration in light with the sudden snow.
It would have happened anyway,
that variation in mood after you had to go.
But was it by chance or, somehow, arranged
that when you left, even the light changed?

## Spring Cleaning

A dry-fly, cobweb morning
sweeping butterfly-winged cocoons
of spun greyness from corners
of window-frames and creases of curtains
at the end of the winter
in the sooty dampness
of the summer cottage
with its calor-gas scented,
wood-smoke permeated dresser and beams.
Green films of mould wiped from the table,
white crinkles of mould from the settles,
black smears of mould from the kitchen cupboard.

A morning of plastic bowls and dustpans,
the clatter of the mop-bucket
and the wringing-out of cloths.
The cleaning, as all cleaning, is unfinished
but now I have collapsed
in the sudden dazzle of sunshine
outside the dark, cool dairy
and the slate-floored parlour,
half-wanting to wade into the mountain stream's
deep pool below the waterfall across the field,
half-dreading the burning sting of iced water.

An earthy morning with the discomforts
and temporary satisfactions
of earth and its incompleteness.
I close lifted eyes to the light,
my all-year home, my roof, my base,
that solid real unmoving place.

## To Rachel, Just Born

Welcome back to earth,
tiny curled-up person,
unbelievable creation
half an hour from birth,
with long fingers wandering
round your face, and mouth
sideways stretching and shaping
in an earnest quest
to find your mother's breast.

When you turn your gaze
to my face hovering
in eager admiration,
your eyes hold the glaze
of dark lakes in still,
remote and age-old mountains.
From their steady depths
they watch and consider me
with benign maturity.

Later, if you find
on waking all is dark
or a meaningless medley of noise
and image, do not mind -
a small cry, a stir
will bring a murmur of words,
the rich smell of skin,
firm arms stilling,
warm milk filling.

This is the world of learning -
do you remember? Dark
shadows, seemingly pointless
jostling and change and turning.
But underneath - don't
be afraid - reality
remains secure, warm,
uplifting, still complete.
Feel its hold, its heartbeat.

## Moment at Blaen Glasffrwd

Carrying a chair into the sun
outside the farmhouse casually
as swallows loop among the barns,
I glance around and see
my son painting in shiny black
the woodshed's corrugated iron walls
as a buzzard overhead
wheels and peers and calls.

The dog pants in the warm grass
and my daughter carries halter
and carrot down the field
to the old horse. I would not alter
a detail or a gesture
in this natural dance,
this sudden fusion of movement
in a link of brilliant chance.

Sitting down in the sun I'm part
of a multi-sided snapshot –
domestic, unexceptional,
unposed, without a plot,
that doesn't even try
to compose itself into a memory –
yet the kind of wealth
a life is compensated by.

# Art and Music

*Listening to music and looking at paintings have been great pleasures in my life, though literature is the only art form I have studied in any depth. In particular my daughter is a professional harpist so for many years we were fortunate to have our home full of her music.*

## After a visit to an Art Gallery

A sitting girl, her face hidden,
dries her dark hair with a blue towel.

Flowing spine and bending neck round up
to the curve of a sea's swell, over
and down the long funnelling slopes
the long towelling drapes.

Jerky angulation
of pointed elbow, wrist,
shoulder, scissor-snaps
at the sight.

Through half-closed eyes
she bobs awash in water-colour haze
or, dusted with pastel, dries.

In her strained stance, compelling tension;
the frenzied towel's descending pressure
stayed by the rising force of firm-positioned feet.

From the back
(undulating tent with outlined ridge-pole)
she is all back.

The front,
a damp, soft mass of blue - rich
Pacific creased with shadows;
flashes of flesh;
and hair, shining and straying,
filaments of varnished weed.

Zoom in on pointillism of tufted towel
or,
to a distant height withdrawn,
dismiss her with a pair of brushstrokes.

Spin and halt
colour, texture, angle
and recompose her rubbing vigour
in balanced cubist tangle.

Quickly, before the finishing
of drying, brushing, dressing,
place her within imagined frames,
shower her with shade,
flatten or elongate.
Observe, stare, discover
uniqueness multiplying
and how
by daze and surfeit of the sight alone
a laden life is brimmed.

## Listening to Music at Home

High with hills the room piles
sky spills on the carpet
mirrors fill with still grey pools.

Massing clouds of chords process
tall through attentive air
fall away in the broad whiteness of walls.

A quick flicker of fire excites
candlesticks, bright fire tongs, prints
that tilt, jig a little, catch light.

Walls swaying, corners widening
and tightening up. In and out
of the picture-glass the lamp pivots and swings.

A gloom of silence now. I wait,
watch the gold and turquoise fade,
the shine become opaque, the room bow out

## The Harpist Describes her Harp

Not an instrument, but a presence.
Not used, but lending itself for music.

Its undulating line a perfect landscape
of hill and valley, gilded and formalised.

It consents to lean against my shoulder,
touch my knee, stooping with heavy grace.

It offers its sensitivities
of flavoured sound to my savouring fingertips.

The side of my head, the inner coils
of my static ear start to vibrate, to murmur.

The clear accuracy of its notes,
the precise division of its lengthening strings

stretching like gentle waves
glinting out of focus, satisfy

the mind, in daily practice and studies,
like a game of chess or balancing an equation.

As I seat myself each day,
it requires me to be steady, calm, true.

A harp trembles at violence.
A string can snap at a flash of irritation.

But the warmth of wood in the curved hollow
of the soundboard can stream with a sap of harmony.

I sense the cells of the tuned wood
unifying into links of light.

And then, as my arms flow and conjure
sound, together we make rivers and downpours,

materialise the moon, the sunlight,
the unfurling of fire and smoke's cadences,

the stir of leaves, the gale-bending
of branches; from nature, creating more than nature.

And more than any composer dreamed
in his brain's greyness. I play, I comprehend, I grow,

I feel. Stirred to tune my own
humanity to match my harp's ideal.

## Impressionist Music in the Summer Woods

Back from the concert hall,
our brains ringing and resounding
with Ravel, Debussy, Stravinsky;
still stirred by the skills
of the orchestra combining
to draw pictures of sound
in the focussed minds of their listeners,
we decided suddenly
to go into the woods.

Ten o'clock on a June
night and still twilight
and a brown owl beating
across our path into
the strumming of trees.
Townspeople daring to step into
someone else's territory,
with only half a moon
conducting the night sky.

Bats dived and fluttered
at us at the edge
of the trees and we stopped
even our whispering
as we pushed into the blackness,
gingerly sensing outwards,
caught up in the interlacing
branches of another
unfamiliar concerto.

Attuned to music, our ears
translated a scuffle of leaves
as the plucking of a cello string
and a high-pitched squeak – perhaps
a mouse – as a lone flute
starting a new movement.
Our own careful footsteps
over twigs and tree roots
burst like explosions.

Then, peering upwards
as if from the front of the stalls,
the owl entered our vision
again, huge and dark,
close, beating its wings
low along a gap
between trees in a silence
that looked louder
than bass drums.

Ravel, Debussy, Stravinsky
and now this masterpiece
of sound and soundlessness
with the perfect timing
of its great performer.
Another variation
on my life's theme –
my straining to comprehend
its brilliant immanent composer.

## The Musician's Absence

The house is dead. No music playing.
Those of us left, restless, shifting
from room to room. We want them back –
those wretched scales and exercises,
familiar cadences curtailed expletively;
the odd, insistent, slightly varied
notes of the tuning-up; vibration
through the walls and door-frames;
change of pace to different rhythms.
Our breathing lacks a tempo set for it
from the daily drama of chords and discords.

Writing is so silent in creation.
It also has its flows and pauses,
its good days when the words
fall neatly under the hand,
its setbacks overcome by bloodymindedness
and sheer persistence, the achievement
of its own self-imposed grades.
But no one else is made aware of them.
It is a huddled introverted occupation
and the final composition is performed
perfunctorily straight to the reader's brain.

Musicians are exposed at every stage
of the jagged graph of their pursuit
of temporary perfection.
Their failures set the house wincing,
but then there are the days of harmony.
And now a power-cut, a sudden deafness.
We have to wait for the end
of the serial we grumbled at.
Life is unbalanced, handicapped.
The resentment that we used to feel
when we woke to the morning practice
and buried our heads under the duvets
was nothing to our present perturbation.

For who would choose silence
in exchange for resonance,
or prefer the lack of dissonance
to the chance of melody?

Taverner's Music

(after hearing "The Hidden Treasure")

A string quartet
sustaining the strain
of unbearable striving
to attain
the exquisite
infinite sweetness,
shading into pain,
of Paradise,
at the end of human stretch,
in opaquely inaudible fog,
when all is a held breath
for the waiting to end,
for the tension to end,
for the earth and the body to end

and the touch beyond the skin
and the sound beyond the sound
to crescendo faintly in.

## Transparent Musicians

You can hear through their music to their souls.
Breath, fingering, eyes.
Their very virtuosity
highlights and heightens
their naked luminosity.

A fingertip on keyboard or on string
says everything
in its exact angle and pressure of touch.
Character, mood, health
unveiled through pause and pitch.

Prolonging intervals by milliseconds
can declare
experience like a lie-detector.
Slightly sharpening a note
can lay the player bare.

Tenderness, passion cannot be faked.
The resonance
of the instrument only enhances
whatever is there or absent.
Yet this defencelessness seems so unfair.

How do intelligent, sensitive humans
ever dare to mount
a platform, invite our focus on themselves
as filters of patterned sound,
let their fault-lines be so plainly found?

Music, instrument, skill, selves,
all on display,
all offered, hungrily consumed
and sometimes carelessly rejected.
Is it pure self-sacrifice that makes them play?

Framed-glass musicians, unable
like the rest of us
to hide behind opaqueness,
mediums for living and dead alike,
open windows, unshuttered to sound's light.

# Miscellaneous Poems

## Welsh Learner

In Tregaron library at an old
school desk, twice a week, I'm learning Welsh.
Conversations between Fred, a learner,
and Sandra Jones of Carmarthen, who is forward
enough to ask him out with her (though married).

My motivation is to find some words
that link me to the ruined barns of heathered
hill-farms, the rusting gates tied up with twine,
the dark blankets of forestry thrown on the landscape
and mini-slagheaps of Bronze Age burial mounds.

I want the words for how it feels to drive
for shopping past the abbey
where Dafydd ap Gwilym is buried, and a stream
beside the road pours down so wastefully
I feel I ought to go and turn it off.

I'm sure there is a way of speaking, beyond me
at the moment, which encompasses
the closed-down chapels and empty petrol-stations,
the red kite swooping low across the lane
and the greening of the larches in the spring.

Welsh words for the black silence at night
apart from the slight hum which is either the fridge
or the river bounding down at the base of the field;
for the curling scent of the woodsmoke, and snapshots
of snowy hills on the way to the Post Office.

At present I'm confused by the different kinds
of Yes and No, the mutated consonants
and the genders of nouns. But I'm pressing on, stumbling,
mispronouncing my Rs and double Ls,
forgetting to start my sentences with verbs.

So that one day I'll see the shadows of clouds
creasing across the hills, and find the exact
light and shade of Welsh to fix them with.
And when the sheep get in my garden again
I'll yell at them in language they understand.

## Sniffing the Spirits

Racing ecstatically along the track,
the dog suddenly brakes
and is pulled in visibly back
to a clump of bushes, one bush,
a particular twig she savours
with her nose - that tool
of extra-sensory perception,
investigating delicately
to test for truth or mischievous deception.

As if a whistle blew or flare
flashed out halting the charge,
diverting the drilled troops elsewhere
in a pre-arranged manoeuvre.
From a patch of old bracken,
a chewed stick on the path,
a gatepost or corner of hedge or wall
she feels the magnetic ray,
hears and obeys at once the silent call.

A medium half in trance,
she tunes in to another plane;
for her the whole walk is a seance
where, clair-nasal, she sniffs up
messages from the spirits
of previous canine travellers.
And I am left bewildered as I go,
clumping on my earthbound course.
This is beyond the literal realms I know.

I look over my shoulder and around.
No sign of this strange
interfusing world to which she's bound.
I go my way blindfolded,
ignorant of the language
she responds to. Her eyes
fill with compassion at my deprivation.
I see the old familiar path ahead.
She follows ley-lines into revelation.

## Truant

I just walked out.
Bells jangled; people pushed and scurried.
Briefcases, legs and games-kits bumped and dodged.
Like a badly edited film the pictures jumped and grated.
My identity was jostled; the pressure clenched inside.
I just walked out.

No one stopped me.
It all came clear, like a maths problem solved at last
after hours of baffled frustration. From cloying heat
and murky confusion, I stepped into this cold sunshine.
I stood out suddenly, distinct and separate,
yet no one stopped me.

A still hub I am
in all a wheel of rush; the only person in this town
conscious of his own breath, deliberately smelling soil
and feeling with wonder his satisfactory weight
on the rough and rusty brick of a solid wall.
So still I am.

There is no anger
on either side, only lack of comprehension.
To walk right out is beyond their bounds,
extra-curricular, so uncontrolled by bells and rules
that it no longer acts as an affront
to rouse their anger.

I have no answers
for their wise advice, their real concern
offered in the corners of cloakrooms. I have no idea
what will become of me. I only know that my reward
is now, not years away. But, for the future,
they have the answers.

They pity me.
They wave their battered books with anxious eagerness
in bare and chalky rooms, and feel assured
they lead the only worthwhile way. I understand
their kind bewilderment, but pity them more
than they pity me.

## Samaritans

Being you was hard. I'm tired tonight.
Yet nothing less would do.

I sensed you would have shrunk at once
from pity's patronage or kindly competence.

At such despair, I felt I had to wrench myself
from here and join you there;

forget my practised calm, my careful words,
and merge mutely into your clenched alarm

until at last your vacuum sucked me down
and for a moment I could say, aghast,

"Yes, I see. There really is no point in going on."
You knew I shared your horror equally.

From my own pain my eyes reached up in need.
It was over then. I was myself again.

You left after a while, and as you pressed my arm,
arranging to meet again, we both managed a smile

## Decorative Initial

Illuminated in this one initial,
all life is interlaced,
all the whorls of myths and beasts
and holiness in which we're placed.

Before the linear logic of the words
the eyes draw down to focus
deep in the convoluted curves
of one coiled, springing flourish.

A monk's miniature vision
flaring up, before he penned
the prescribed words with precision
to the gospel story's end.

An occupation for the mind
and curb on the wandering gaze.
Stop. Hold. Be still. It commands
at the doorway to the page.

From the illusion of horizontal
time is seen ascending
the crowded ladder of the vertical,
space and time transcending.

At the same starting point re-starting,
there is no separation;
the dead return; distant and future
loved ones form one generation.

There is no history, but only now,
and future mere delusion.
Only the ever-unfolding present
exists, containing all in fusion.

I am the letter and the manuscript.
I am the sacred word;
the scribe, the vellum and the colour,
the man, the serpent and the bird.

Embossed in gold, the spiral bank
of pattern intertwines;
no history but now – a blank
page and infinite designs.

## Coming of Age

When Arthur drew the sword out of the stone
it slipped into his grip with oiled precision.
His strength was needed not to pull it out
but bear with total clarity of vision
the sombre implications of the act
which made him long to leave the sword intact.

As all eyes watched him and the silence fell
outside the Chapel on that autumn day,
distractedly he waded in a dream
through fallen leaves, his mind in disarray;
exulting in his hour and yet rebelling,
freedom resisting, destiny compelling.

He had come of age. The blossom of the spring
spread carefree on the grass had gone. The fruit
must now be picked, or left to windfall waste.
History allowed no substitute.
Only he could harvest all their longing,
produce a crop from all the wars and wronging.

He drew the sword with flourish and with fire,
but felt in fullness all the weight of loss;
out of dependence he must draw himself,
and with the jewelled prize accept a cross.
Through the triumphal arch he knew he'd find
the gates of earlier safety slammed behind.

Excalibur soared in a shining arc
and severed off his past – bright falcon days,
the hectic chaos of the hunt, songs
and distant talk of wars heard through a haze,
nights beside the fire of sleepy laughter,
wine within and not a thought for after.

Now there was no chance to slip away,
to merge into the shadows, disengage,
take the protection nurse must give to child,
guardian to growing ward, or knight to page.
Now alone he had to take control,
be king to people, land and his own soul.

Merlin's power wrapped round him like a cloak,
Merlin's knowledge that this had to be,
Merlin's promise blazed in dragon skies
and dazzling in the sword for all to see,
but he must rise to meet it, bear the strain,
fully stretch his powers to hold and reign.

Handling the moulded hilt, he also felt
the grip of realism and grim acceptance,
a sinking of the heart as each man knelt,
grief with the pride. He gave a wistful glance
at the free sky and out along the track
into the wild forest, leading back.

## Merlin

Merlin is waking in this ancient land,
long sleep forsaking.
His breathing deepens.
He stirs a withered hand.

From him the rounds of stars and seasons flow.
His the spring within the seed we sow.
For him the great oak forests stretch and grow.
His summer staff the snake winds warmly round.
With harvest chaff his spirit spreads the ground.
In autumn frost for him the berries glow
ruby as blood in the wild hedgerow.
His is the winter pearl of mistletoe
and thorn that casts its petals on the snow.

Merlin is waking in this ancient land,
long sleep forsaking.
His breathing deepens.
He stirs a withered hand.

We wait in longing for his waking hour.
He sends his gales ahead to cleanse and scour.
The earth is heaving under town and tower.
Blasted trees with branches white as bone
burst out in leaves to make his wizard's throne.
In henge and circle, over ridge and moor
his chakras open into petalled flower.
His blood is running through the lines of power
and beacons shout their messages in fire.

Merlin is waking in this ancient land,
Long sleep forsaking.
His breathing deepens.
He stirs a withered hand.

He marks his coming in the fields of corn
in runic signs to which we wake at morn.
From devic kingdoms are his forces drawn,
who marshal silently to work his will
still as the frost they form on copse and hill.
To honour earth these hidden knights have sworn,
proudly unbroken like the unicorn.
They wait the summons of his ancient horn,
the age of alchemy that must be born.

Merlin is waking in this ancient land,
long sleep forsaking,
His breathing deepens.
He stirs a withered hand.

His cloak is ragged with the centuries,
but nature gladly trusts his wise decrees.
His tide of strength is rising with the seas.
The soaring hawk that leaps from heavy land,
the pouring holy well, the healing hand
carry the magic of his energies.
The inner lights of moon and sun increase,
the Arthur in the human heart he frees
and wakes our crystal creativities.

Merlin is awake
here in this land.
Your dreams and lethargy forsake.
Wait his command.

## Chiron the Centaur

To be a horse is to be at one with earth,
to widen out; for hooves on living turf
are alive to all sensation,
beat with the earth's vibration.
The weighty onrush of a falling stream
as you are trotting by can shiver through
your muscles, make you strain
to toss cascading mane
and stretch and pour in waterfalls of strength.
The rising sap of forests makes your blood
surge faster, your branching veins
beat like hurricanes
among the treetops; your skin thickens like bark
and mane scatters behind like gusts of leaves.
On rocky hills you ring
and resonate, echoing
and belling messages for miles. Hillsides
of boulders are chambers of sound to us;
stones, seemingly inert
to humans, make us alert
and sharp as crystal as we travel through.
And to gallop on a windy day is to use
the whipping reeds, the racing
clouds, the forward-chasing
trees as a power house. As you thud the ground,
they write your poems for you, they sing your songs.
The earth is your sustenance,
your breath; its live expanse
an extension of yourself. Have you seen us toss
our hooves, break rhythm, vary our intervals of tread?
This is how we play,
teasing ourselves this way
by the contrast of tantalising separations
with conscious renewal, till we can bear no more,
luxuriate and roll
and flood ourselves with the whole
scent and touch of her pulsations.

To be a horse is to sense without a thought,
like a beat below a tune,
the patterns of the moon
and where each day the sun is in the sky;
to absorb the magnetism of planets
direct like a fire's glow
or sunlight bouncing slow
off a seam of quartz at noonday; is to cross a line
of power or stream deep underground and feel
at once its depth and length,
its history and strength,
the intenseness of its light and dark; is to see
a human's thinking in the colours round it;
its calmness or its tension,
its flashes of dissension;
is to wince, as if struck, at the flash of its fear;
is to find the smell of sickness overpowering
in one still feeling well,
and in advance to tell
the approach of death and watch its deep blue peace
reach out, enclose and settle everything.

When I am wholly horse,
pure essence of lean force,
I am a drummer of earth, a proud dominant
in the chord of the landscape.
I cleft the air with my canter.
Like a mountain river I swerve
and switch, a current of nerve.
I hold my spine high like a skyline.
I leap with verve and fly over rocks and walls
like the arrow-flight of a swift,
all swoop and graceful lift.
My power shines through my skin, whoops in my heart,
and builds up like a reservoir, rising
and rising till the hurl,
the flurry and the whirl
of a pelting gallop is needed to undam me.

I live for the instant that contains all.
I am the near and far –
the faintest, distant star
and the heather at my hoof. I am free, as humans
never are. And when I change back to my brain,

it is colourless abstraction,
reality's contraction,
dimness and dry streambeds of thought again,
a world with ideas for its elements. Human words
need twenty meanings more,
together with a store
of sounds and smells for each, and different tastes
of grass before I truly could begin
to tell you how I feel –
and then your brain would reel,
quickly swirl and clog at all the input
of this range of senses, as mine did
until I came to learn
how instantly to turn
from mind to body at will – as now I must.

After all this talk, I have to rise and press
my hooves into the soil,
flinging away the toil
of language. I must shake and stretch my body,
walk and trot a little, breathe the signals
of the sheening air,
strong, alive, aware,
then break out in a running canter, rear,
buck a little and set off, spring off … .anywhere.

# INDEX